Desire and the Sign

Desire

and the Sign

Nineteenth-Century American Fiction

FRED G. SEE

Louisiana State University Press
Baton Rouge and London

Copyright © 1987 by Louisiana State University Press
All rights reserved
Manufactured in the United States of America

10 9 8 7 6 5 4 3 2 1

Designer: Christopher Wilcox
Typeface: Sabon
Typesetter: G & S Typesetters, Inc.
Printer: Thomson-Shore, Inc.
Binder: John Dekker & Sons, Inc.

Several chapters of this book are revised versions of articles that have appeared in journals. The author wishes to thank the editors at Queens College Press for permission to reprint "The Kinship of Metaphor: Incest and Language in Melville's *Pierre*," which was published in *Structuralist Review* (Fall, 1978); the Regents of the University of California for permission to reprint "The Demystification of Style: Metaphoric and Metonymic Language in *A Modern Instance*" © 1974, which was published in *Nineteenth-Century Fiction*, Vol. XXVIII, No. 4; the editors at Wayne State University Press for permission to reprint "*Sister Carrie* and the Lost Language of the Heart," which was published in *Criticism*, Vol. XX, No. 2 (1978), 144–66; and the editors of Johns Hopkins University Press for permission to reprint "Henry James and the Art of Possession," which appeared in *American Realism: New Essays*, edited by Eric Sundquist.

Library of Congress Cataloging-in-Publication Data

See, Fred G., 1937–
    Desire and the sign.

    Includes bibliographical references and index.
    1. American fiction—19th century—History and
criticism. 2. Desire in literature. 3. Semiotics
and literature. I. Title.
PS374.D38S44   1987   813'.3'09   86-21088
ISBN 0-8071-1313-1

To Fred and Dorothy See

CONTENTS

ACKNOWLEDGMENTS

I began this study at the suggestion of Henry Nash Smith, whose careful and generous advice was always exemplary. I wish he could have lived to see its final form; his learning and his influence were always clarifying. Later many friends and colleagues helped me keep sane as I struggled to compose my book and myself. For this I am grateful to Jim Bunn, Bob Daly, Bill Fischer, Dick Fly, Joe Riddel, and Herb Schneidau; and to Gale Carrithers and Ed Dryden, who read the entire manuscript and made many important suggestions. Geoff Walsh gave special assistance during a difficult period, and helped me to understand a number of handicaps which stood in the way. My typist, Rita Keller, showed remarkable patience and understanding. My son Jared was always invigorating. And above all it is a pleasure to thank my wife, Bonnie, who read every draft and made me see the way to improve it: the best of this work is hers too.

I want also to express my gratitude to the Research Foundation of the State University of New York, whose support enabled the research of several portions of this study.

Desire and the Sign

In an essay called "Where to Begin?" Roland Barthes meditates on the difficulty of initiating any analysis of literature. Much, Barthes says, stands in the way of beginning: unruly divergencies make their various claims on one's confidence; there is the temptation to expect, or much worse to find, an unqualified explanation of the text, "a final signified which would be the work's truth or its determination"; anyone beginning feels, perhaps, an urge to control the variety of the text by postulating a "canonical" unity, both of meaning and of method—it is a little like falling in love.

Barthes' meditation perfectly understands the difficulties of remaining free of the numberless, exclusive claims with which readings encircle texts. And it proposes, it seems to me, exactly the solution one comes to discover only after one's work is finished, after the atrocious problem of writing has been suspended—that is, how one meant to begin all along, what one wished to have known at the outset: "that it is a matter of entering, by analysis . . . into the play of the signifier, into the writing: in a word, to accomplish, by [one's] labor, the text's plural."[1]

1. Roland Barthes, "Where to Begin?" in his *New Critical Essays*, trans. Richard Howard (New York, 1980), 79.

Just so: to realize that the text is ludic; to find the text's plural by allowing the signifier its play—its oscillation, and its deployment: to begin by accepting the sign's own imagination—what one really discovers only in being seduced: "the sign develops, uncoils at the same time that it is interpreted," Gilles Deleuze says, just as "the jealous lover develops the possible worlds enclosed within the beloved."[2] This means finding the interior of the sign, seeing its structure as well as its shape, its latent as well as manifest motive. For me this has meant Saussure's sign, the mutuality of paired opposites, signifier and signified, the sensible and conceptual aspects of the sign; not an object but an energy which might be re-stated as the contest between the fragments and the integrity of meaning— reality in ruins, or reality whole.

I assume, then, that the sign is systematically double. According to Saussure, the sign exists only through the association of signifier and signified. Whenever only one element is retained, "the entity vanishes. . . . We constantly risk grasping only a part of the entity and thinking that we are embracing it in totality." By way of analogy he suggests "a chemical compound like water, a combination of hydrogen and oxygen; taken separately, neither element has any of the properties of water."[3] In *Specimen Days* Whitman puts his sense of the "literary attempt" in remarkably similar terms when he recalls an early fascination with "The sea-shore—that suggesting, dividing line, contact, junction, the solid marrying the liquid . . . blending the real and ideal, and each made portion of the other."[4] The sign, in other words, is the intercourse of its own differences, an alliance of opposites as well as an irreducible structure. Being both, it is clear but not simple. The sign is a marginal relationship; it expresses a nuclear bonding of the fragments and the idea of a universe. This is one sense in which it is plural. Moreover, this plurality tends to become apparent over time, a dimension in which

2. Gilles Deleuze, *Proust and Signs,* trans. Richard Howard (New York, 1973); 89. Deleuze also speaks of the "pluralistic" system of signs, 83–91.

3. Ferdinand de Saussure, *Course in General Linguistics,* trans. Wade Baskin, ed. Charles Bally and Albert Sechehays (New York, 1966), 102–103.

4. Walt Whitman, *Specimen Days,* ed. John Kouwenhaven (New York, 1950), 650.

the sign is subject to changes—in history the order of signs is mutable.

Besides, the sign's opposition balances possibilities which are always in the process of being negotiated, and the context of this negotiation is immense. For Lévi-Strauss the "dichotomizing character" of the sign is to be found in, and explains, the logic of classifications which allows rational and unreasoning aspects of reality to co-exist as a systematic totality.[5] This makes possible a comprehensible relation of Nature on the one hand and Culture on the other. Without this we could scarcely live in our world. Jacques Derrida evolves something very similar from Saussure: "the system of signs is constituted," he says, "by the difference between the terms. . . . the elements of signification function not by virtue of the compact force of their cores but by the network of oppositions that distinguishes them and relates them to one another," and this gives rise to the alliance of presence and absence, the notion of difference, and the "systematic play" of that difference, which creates "the possibility of conceptuality, of the conceptual system of process in general."[6] In *Violence and the Sacred* and "*To Double Business Bound*" Réné Girard understands spontaneous sacrifice, which establishes the fundamental categories of Same and Different, to generate exactly this same symbolicity; and Jacques Lacan observes that Freud's mechanisms of primary process thinking, "in which the unconscious assumes its rule, correspond exactly to . . . the signifier's effects of substitution and combination," and, moreover, "that the slightest alteration in the relation between man and the signifier . . . changes the whole course of history by modifying the moorings that anchor his being." Indeed in concluding an essay on the questions and values "at the very heart of analytic practice" Lacan says "if you want to know more, read Saussure . . . who can truly be said to be the founder of modern linguistics."[7]

5. Claude Lévi-Strauss, *The Savage Mind,* trans. unacknowledged (Chicago, 1966), 159 and Chaps. 5 and 6.

6. Jacques Derrida, "Differance," in his *Speech and Phenomena,* trans. David B. Allison (Evanston, 1973), 139.

7. Jacques Lacan, "The subversion of the subject and the dialectic of desire in the

These theories of classification, ideation, symbolicity, and consciousness (at bottom all are really theories of Culture) derive alike from Saussure's formulation of the sign. There is even an important analysis of literary history predicated on this semiotics of opposing mutuality: Jakobson's notation that romantic language is metaphoric and realist language metonymic.[8] And this possibility has been magnified in Foucault's studies of epochal patterns of signification. In part these manifold dimensions of Saussure's sign suggest what is meant by the plurality of the text: that the entire network of human systems, both their origin and their historical development, must be implied in the textual activity, since all have their common evolution from the sign and all depend identically—and isomorphically—from its structure: as the law of signs admits change, so do the systems of human thought.

This is the model I have found most useful, because most ample; and if I seem to be invoking a pantheon it is only because I need to suggest how the model I am using implies the range and importance of textual plurality, and its possible relationship to the forces which, according to this recent critical idiom, inaugurate and sustain human civilization and history. That said I will generally tend to set aside the theoretical details of this vast claim and turn directly toward something much more modest, a reading of the texts in which this plurality is manifest. Or rather, to be as specific as possible, toward certain texts which I understand to be representative of the sign's pluralizing activity over a historical period. I wish to examine the changing status of literary signs in a particular time and place—in American fiction, roughly in the second half of the nineteenth century, when romanticism gave way to the realist endeavor.

All the larger applications of the sign according to Saussure will be useful to me, each theoretical dimension will always be germane

---

Freudian unconscious," "The agency of the letter or reason since Freud," and "The Freudian Thing, or the meaning of the return to Freud in Psychoanalysis," in his *Ecrits*, trans. Alan Sheridan (New York, 1977), 298, 174, 118–25.

8. Roman Jakobson, "Two Aspects of Language and Two Types of Linguistic Disturbances," in Roman Jakobson and Morris Halle (eds.), *Fundamentals of Language* (The Hague, 1956). Subsequent references will be given parenthetically in the text.

(it could hardly be otherwise if all our systems function under the sign's law), but I will need most to assume Jakobson's version, since that concerns itself with evidence that is more empirically accessible than, say, the lost original rift between Nature and Culture. I want to understand the exemplary relationship of romanticism and realism not simply as a historical development, though it certainly is that, but as evidence of the sign's structure. To what extent, then, does literary history reflect the sign's mediation of its own differences? Not: literary history is *only* the record of the sign's structure, but: to *what extent* does the law of the sign govern literary history? From the founding of American culture the sign had been oriented toward the signified, the plane of spirit and the soul. Metaphorically, it bridges and unites different orders of reality. But sometime in the nineteenth century the sign begins to reorient itself toward signifiers—toward an order which conceived itself as fragments rather than essential unity. It is romanticism which examines the ideal dimension of meaning, and which is "closely linked with metaphor," Jakobson points out; and he goes on to note "the equally intimate ties of realism with metonymy" (81), with details, freeplay, and debris.

Both tendencies, the movement through metaphor to the ideal site of meaning and the gaze across a metonymic scene, which accepts the priority of fragments, are always genetically present in the sign; either the signified or the signifier tends to predominate. By focusing on this literary dichotomy, in which the plurality of the sign insists on revealing itself, I hope to be able to discuss the movement of the sign's structure through time.

Of the various possible subjects of the novels I take as representative, I have selected desire as most likely to demonstrate this structure. Some such selection is necessary in order to focus the sign's pressure consistently, and besides, it is in desire that the sign most clearly dramatizes its doubleness and its internal contention. Desire invariably requires the sign to deploy its opposing powers to their fullest extent, perhaps that is the best way to say it. This cannot fail to put formal (or sedimented) balances at risk. Leo Bersani, for example, suggests that "desire is a threat to the form of realistic fiction. Desire can subvert social order; it can also disrupt novelistic order. . . . In formal terms, disruptive desire could be thought of as a disease of disconnectedness in a part of the structure which rejects being defined by its relations to other parts and asserts, as it were, a scandalous affinity with elements alien to the structure." Desire attracts, magnetizes, repolarizes the sign—it makes the order and discourse of the sign problematic; it compels a reorientation. Thus, Bersani goes on to point out, the hero of desire "is an intruder in a world of significantly related structures, of unambiguous beginnings and definitive conclusions," and in such a situation we should expect the sign's responses to be articulated very clearly.[9]

Indeed it is the nature of desire to seek a radical change in any pattern of relationships, that is in any structure, and not only in fiction—the paradigms of imagination are implicated too, we are all implicated, and it is helpful to add a conclusion of Foucault's, which clarifies Bersani's suggestion and provides the discourse of desire with a wider scene:

> With the great series of binary oppositions (body/soul, flesh/spirit, spirit, instinct/reason, drives/consciousness) that seemed to refer sex to a pure mechanics devoid of reason, the West has managed not only, or not so much, to annex sex to a field of rationality, which would not be all that remarkable an achievement, seeing how accustomed we are to such "conquests" since the Greeks, but to bring us almost entirely—our bodies, our minds, our individuality, our history—under the sway of a logic of concupiscence and desire. Whenever it is a question of knowing who we are, it is this logic that henceforth serves as our master key.[10]

The logic of desire is the master key to understanding—over the last several centuries at least, during which sexuality, "the sign of sex" under which we have "placed ourselves" (78), has become an element of power "endowed with the greatest instrumentality: useful for the greatest number of maneuvers and capable of serving as a point of support, as a linchpin, for the most varied strategies"

9. Leo Bersani, *A Future for Astyanax: Character and Desire in Literature* (Boston, 1976), 66, 67. See also the interesting debate between Bersani and Walter Benn Michaels in *Critical Inquiry*, VIII (1981), 158–71.

10. Michel Foucault, *An Introduction*, trans. Robert Hurley (2 vols.; New York, 1980), 78, Vol. I of *The History of Sexuality*, 2 vols. Subsequent references will be given parenthetically in the text.

(102). Accordingly I will be looking at the signs of desire in five novels written between 1853 and 1900, hoping to find a pattern of deployment, some trace of the operation of structure, in this most promising scene where, as Charles Feidelson has said, we may see the historical beginnings of the process "by which idealism and materialism, romanticism and realism, give way to the symbolistic point of view"—what Feidelson earlier calls "the relationship between thought, word, and object . . . [whose] fulcrum was the problem of mediation, which led to the problem of language."[11] Both signs and language undergo profound discovery and change during the period bounded on either end by Mrs. Stowe and Henry James and including Hawthorne, Melville, Howells, and Dreiser.[12]

Hawthorne I have not dealt with in such sharp focus as my other authors, in spite of his interest as a symbolic writer obsessed with desire, because Melville's deployment of desire and its signs really eclipses what Hawthorne, even in *The Marble Faun,* was able to accomplish. Hawthorne evaded what Melville faced: not only the collapse of systematic meaning, but also the scandalous limits of the new system of signs. From *Twice-Told Tales* to his unfinished fragments, Hawthorne developed a thematics of desire which neither accepted nor repudiated the metaphysical dimension central to the writers of domestic sentiment, like Mrs. Stowe, whose works he famously condemned.[13] Like Dickens he was reluctant either to surrender the transcendent implications of the sentimental vision, or to endorse them fully.

A good example of this ambivalence is "The Old Manse," with its constant escape from the hearth and its constant reaffirmation of domestic values. In spite of "the freedom which we . . . won from all custom and conventionalism and fettering influence of

11. Charles Feidelson, *Symbolism and American Literature* (Chicago, 1953), 214, 70, 4.

12. See Philip F. Gura, "Language and Meaning: An American Tradition," *American Literature,* LIII (1981), 1–21, for a good general description of the context for language philosophy in the nineteenth century.

13. For a recent study of Hawthorne's vexed relationship to the material real and an analysis of his efforts to reflect this relationship in his fiction, see Henry Nash Smith, *Democracy and the Novel: Popular Resistance to Classic Amercian Writers* (New York, 1978), 16–34.

man on man" by visits to wild and uncivilized scenes, Hawthorne says, "I prayed that the upper influences might long protect the institutions that had grown out of the heart of mankind."[14] The statement suggests Hawthorne's vexed relationship to a sentimental intelligence, though it does not explain it.

But Melville's attitude toward institutions and sentiment was more radically interrogative. As F. O. Matthiessen puts it, "The ambiguities between the actual and the ideal were destined to torture him as they never did Hawthorne's steadier, if less adventurous mind";[15] and at this important point in the history of the sign's structure I have found it more useful to emphasize Melville's radical struggle to change the tendency of signification. I know what I risk by this emphasis; but it is undoubtedly Melville who sees and comes to terms with this problem of the sign, not Hawthorne.

So after some introductory discussion of Hawthorne I will move from Mrs. Stowe's sentimental language, in which gratified desire provides a metaphoric incarnation of presence, directly to Melville's fully scandalized language, and then to Howells' metonymic questioning, Dreiser's self-effacing (and self-replenishing) signifiers, and finally James's metaphorics of possession—all of which couple the configuration of signs with an exactly analogous development of the structure of desire. What happens to one happens to the other. This development is not always strictly chronological, however. Melville's attack on signs precedes Mrs. Stowe's reconstitution of meaning when, according to a strict theoretical logic, his attack should follow her inscription of law. Similarly, James's recuperation of metaphor, logically the last movement in the sign's oscillation between extremes, historically precedes Dreiser's efforts to displace metaphor with a purely metonymic reading of desire and signs. Never mind. My readers will understand that any literary development ignores absolute historical calibrations, and is not always perfectly synchronized with designs that only become visible in the wider perspectives afforded by time.

14. William Charvat, Roy Harvey Pearce, and Claude Simpson (eds.), *The Centenary Edition of the Works of Nathaniel Hawthorne* (16 vols. to date; Columbus, 1962–), X, 25, 26.

15. F. O. Matthiessen, *American Renaissance: Art and Expression in the Age of Emerson and Whitman* (New York, 1941), 258.

CHAPTER I

Magic from the Caverns of the Soul

"Indeed a man without sensibility exhibits no sign of a soul."

—*The Power of Sympathy*

No sign of a soul"—what can it mean? This first American novel, published in 1789, looks back over the edifying horrors which it has inscribed for us and for "the FEMALE MIND" of "*United Columbia*" and concludes that without sensibility, the soul cannot be read.[1] Insofar as the soul has a meaning apparent to us, it is manifest because of feeling. Without sensibility, then, there could be no trace of presence. Perhaps, even, meaning would not exist without this matrix of sensibility, which reveals a divine fabrication: "Hail Sensibility!" (we are told unequivocally): "Sweetener of the joys of life! Heaven has implanted thee in the breasts of his children— to soothe the sorrows of the afflicted—to mitigate the wounds of the stranger who falleth in our way" (68).

From heaven to the heart, from the heart to the soul, from the soul to signs—and back again: this is the path of significance taken by our earliest fiction; it is the dimension of all reading: "Blessed is he that readeth," the Bible promises (Revelation 1:3), and perhaps this is why—thanks to sensibility, reading can follow the original path of

1. William Hill Brown, *The Power of Sympathy*, ed. Herbert Ross Brown (Boston, 1961), dedicatory page. Subsequent references will be given parenthetically in the text.

spirit. Text reflects soul, soul mirrors text.[2] The formula is explicitly theological. To be sure, sensibility and sentiment differ in degree; Herbert Ross Brown distinguishes "between conscience and impulse, punctilio and ecstasy."[3] Still, each retains an original affinity with their common source, the Protestant doctrine of the prepared heart: "Hail Sensibility!" (the novel invokes the concept over and over)—"Ye eloquent tears of beauty! . . . it was *these* that opened every avenue of contrition in my heart, when *words* would have damned up every sluice of repentance" (78).[4]

But not the words of the sentimental text. These words constitute a kind of Scripture themselves; they do not "damn"—the misspelling must be deliberate. "Sentiment out of date!" cries a character responding to a pert dismissal of feeling as "unfashionable": "'Sentiment out of date—alas! poor Yorick. . . .' He continued his address to the book [Sterne's *Sentimental Journey*]. . . . 'These anti-sentimentalists would banish thee from the society of all books. . . . eyes have *they,* but they see not—ears have *they,* but they hear not, neither is there any knowledge to be found in them'" (24). One text sanctifies another: this echoes nothing less than the New Testament (Mark 8:18); it is both Christ's rebuke to his doubting disciples, and the rebuke of the master text to a fallen reader. This is not the ambivalent representation "that implies the absence of what is being made present again in writing"; it is a mode which, as Paul de Man allows, "confirms rather than undermines the plenitude" of experience.[5] The sentimental text reawakens, perhaps even creates, sensibility for the reader by representing it, just as Heaven implants sensibility in God's children.

And sensibility thus represented makes the soul manifest. The signs of the sentimental text, the Samaritan text which heals the fallen stranger, nourish a presence within their depths—if one be-

2. For a wider application of the textual formula, see Louis I. Bredvold, *The Natural History of Sensibility* (Detroit, 1961), 23.

3. Herbert Ross Brown, *The Sentimental Novel in America, 1789–1860* (New York, 1959), 74.

4. See Norman Pettit, *The Heart Prepared: Grace and Conversion in Puritan Spiritual Life* (New Haven, 1966), esp. Chap. 1.

5. Paul de Man, "The Rhetoric of Blindness," in his *Blindness and Insight: Essays in the Rhetoric of Contemporary Criticism* (New York, 1971), 123.

lieves. But one did believe, and on into the nineteenth century as well. Soul and sensibility are intertextual; thanks to the sign they converge and exchange a coherent pattern of meaning. They bracket American fiction for nearly a hundred years. There is scarcely any limit to the complexities which gather around this apparently simple structure of opposition. By now Saussure's theory of the sign is well known, but it is worth insisting that the opposition of the two capacities which juxtapose to constitute the sign—signifier and signified—is not fixed. It is useful to think of this relationship as a rivalry, in which one energy or the other predominates under certain conditions (aphasia, psychosis) or in certain cultural contexts (romanticism, realism), or even at certain stages of every speech act (syllable, word). In sentimental fiction the relationship expresses the theological coherence of textuality, since in "sensibility," material and spiritual reality engage. Feeling allows brute instinct to escape its brutality, its horror; the body's sensibility is the sign of something which is as it were always next to itself—the suffering of a mystical body, and of a sacrifice; suffering has an alibi, it is somewhere else: it shares in the sacrificial structure of agony. Suffering is metaphoric, intelligible. Thanks to sensibility, the body transcends its limits, its meaning is displaced into an idea: it becomes a trace, it turns toward an origin—not only of suffering but of signification. The body's own feelings, and therefore the body itself, become a means of grace, according to this function of the sign.

But there are other patterns of dominance, other configurations, areas of (literary) history for example, when signs or texts tend to be typically metonymic rather than metaphoric, deconstructive rather than constitutive—renouncing the plenitude of ideals, seeking to gather up the scattered evidence of order. Romantic language tries, and sometimes succeeds, to refer outside itself, but realism sets out to be self-referential. Sometimes language returns, according to an author's intention or because of its own custom, through metaphor to an origin outside of language, so that language exceeds its limit, expresses a kind of ecstasy—that condition which puts the soul outside the body and its sensibilities, beyond language or the need for language. But language also allows signs to suppress their noumenal referentiality and to become, as a consequence, interred within the phenomenal real. Such a literature of signifiers often sets the detective or the analyst at its center; without such a figure, this reality would become unbearably confused and threatening. Here the sign relentlessly seems to oppose its own blank and unrelated surface to all interpretations. Witness depositions concerning events on board the *San Dominick* (Benito Cereno's slaver), for instance, deliberately turn away from metaphoric possibilities of likeness.[6] Rather they establish the limit of the phenomenal sign and return reading to a sort of paranoid despair, a tendency that marks some postmodern fiction—"See the moon? It hates us," says one of Donald Barthelme's narrators, who goes on to add, "Fragments are the only forms I trust."[7]

So the sign may be exemplified by a theological instance, sensibility, as the point where man's history is revealed as a mythic enactment: "there are no creatures," Cotton Mather says in 1721, "but what are His *Medals*, on every one of them the name of JESUS is to be found inscribed."[8] This point marks the intersection of two tendencies and the privilege of one over the other. The priority of the signified, the noumenal order, places all discrete attributes of experience, all the fragments of our perception and understanding, under the rule of metaphor. But theological orthodoxy is not required in the use of literary signs, nor is the priority of the signified, and this becomes an increasingly important problem from the nineteenth century on. Signs are less and less committed to the special custody of the signified, just as the idea of the soul ceases to be very useful, in literature or anywhere else. The development of a commonsense psychology, for example, made "the term 'soul' . . . its first and most important casualty. To employ this word in a psychological textbook, after 1890, signified either being behind the times or adhering to a neo-scholastic, i.e., Thomistic, dogma."[9] The idea of the soul, with all its ramifications, dissolves and re-

6. See for instance Eric J. Sundquist, "Suspense and Tautology in *Benito Cereno*," *Glyph* 8 (1981), 104–105.

7. Donald Barthelme, "See the Moon?" in his *Unspeakable Practices, Unnatural Acts* (New York, 1969), 156–57.

8. Cotton Mather, "Of Man," in Kenneth B. Murdock (ed.), *Selections from Cotton Mather* (New York, 1926), 355.

9. A. A. Roback, *A History of American Psychology* (New York, 1951), 122–23.

forms as something else, something measurable. What remains intact and compelling is the idea of a tense relationship between the differences which sensibility and the soul once mediated.

This relationship is always being tested. Its power to imply the order of reality continuously faces an ordeal. This is clear in the patterns of literary history, not only in the work of Melville or Barthelme but in Howells and Dreiser, thanks to whose work the sign reestablishes a reign of signifiers: objects, fragments, a debris. Then the signified must be obsessively rediscovered, or expressed as cast loose and lost like the measureless value of the Maltese Falcon, "slipped completely through our fingers," leaving a mesmerizing, worthless body in its place.[10] What is put at the center of Hammett's novel is relentlessly only an image of original value—a substitution of lead for gold, an inversion of the ancient alchemical magic: a division of reality, not a mystical unification. This sign undergoes an immediate analysis, like the desire of Spade for Brigid O'Shaughnessy or of Brigid for Spade, or of Joel Cairo for Wilbur or any of the instances of desire in the novel, all of which (and much more) it implies. It is not the real thing, none of it is; here neither desire nor the sign expresses the marriage of actual and ideal which Hawthorne struggled to achieve; they are revealed to be means of expressing fragmentation, the disjunctiveness of things. They show the extent to which the ideal is only the lost point of a quest become venal, gross, and corrupt, like Casper Gutman. Superficially the falcon resembles its original form but they share no innate identity. It expresses a radical and incurable difference from its original value; it functions according to its attributes—shape, weight, elusiveness—and according to the purely material wealth they seem to measure. And so does Gutman, who replicates the terms under which the Black Bird has meaning: shape, weight, elusiveness, the illusion of great value. The statuette is a sign which ceases before our eyes to be metaphoric. It exposes the danger of metaphor, shows how it can involve us in a mystification—how it can transform quest into detour.[11] It reduces metaphor to irony: it is not, after all, metaphoric; it is metonymic—like the novel's desires, it

10. Dashiell Hammett, *The Maltese Falcon* (New York, 1972), 173.

11. I am indebted of course to Jacques Derrida's "White Mythology," trans. F. C. T. Moore, *New Literary History*, VI (1974), 5–74.

changes nothing; no value or meaning is transferred by its traverse across the text. The Maltese Falcon dramatizes structure as the signs of sensibility had done; but in this instance we see the polarity of signification reverse, and the universe of meaning change.

Often enough culture relies on literary texts to declare the order of its signs, as if literature were a nomenclator—the servant who calls out names and relationships for his master. Literature is no slave to culture, to be sure, but it may be culture's voice. It serves to identify values at large, and for Hammett it introduces icons, consciousness, texts—even language—as the objects of an ultimate, ontological fragmentation. In realist fiction this is often indicated by the deadening of sensibility, its replacement by an irreducible sexuality which can only be known as ironic, mechanistic, devouring; not sensibility but hysteria or despair, sadistic hostility, masochism: Temple Drake. What was emotion as the sign of a Passion is now, at the most, a longing for something lost: neither sensibility nor sentiment but simply desire, the discourse of what is missing.

So the larger design of meaning in American fiction may be seen as an oscillation which follows the sign's structure, a relationship of paired opposites which is always evident, not only in literature but in the other, isomorphic structures which sound the chord of culture. The relationship is always negotiating the equilibrium of all the systems depending on the sign—everything within culture, everything under the rule of law, everything across from nature: consciousness, language, literature, everything hominized as René Girard says, are all part of the same text, a ferment whose catalyst is neither signifier nor signified but the opposition between them.[12]

Little distorts the sign but madness and nothing can force it outside the law which is encoded in its structure, comprising that structure. Imagination shifts it, but the sign is placid and changes slowly. It may be made unstable, however, like all order, by scandal—by a gross violation. Or rather—for what does scandal mean at its root?—by the trap into which, thanks to an enemy's snare, one stumbles, or springs. The word derives from the same root as "scan," scrutiny, discernment (criticism, perhaps): the pattern or

12. René Girard, "*To Double Business Bound*" (Baltimore, 1978), 216.

analysis of metrical feet (so that they might not fall into the enemy's trap). To examine, test, criticize—at the beginning of this word, in some luminous moment of insight, the concept of scandal fused two meanings, entrapment and understanding. To put it another way, scandal is an entrapment that requires to be understood, an offense or error which makes it possible to see the necessity and hidden structure of law, an outrage which undoes law and rhythm and calls forth an original clarity of regulation: the cadence of language.

Can signs be scandalized too? Remember, sensibility was implanted "to mitigate the wounds of the stranger who falleth in our way." The signs of sensibility, of an understanding which is seamlessly metaphorical, countermand the injuries of the scandalous falling stranger, whose erratic career threatens to test our faith to its undoing. Sensibility and scandal are the opposite capacities of language, and of desire: they cause the annealment and the fragmentation of significance. And sensibility, up until the middle of the nineteenth century (and in lowbrow "romances," up until the present day), was always manifest as law—a law so homogeneous and sedimented that scandal is required to make it reflect upon its own order. So Melville and Hawthorne realized, though Melville stood more openly for scandal, and more resolutely against the sentimental canon epitomized by Mrs. Stowe. He and she constitute the brackets of literary signifying; one could scarcely go farther toward either extreme without finding sheer decadence or bare formula; and Hawthorne, whose texts aim but fail to scandalize the system of literary signs, falls somewhere between—not in terms of any criterion of excellence, naturally, but in terms of his failure either to release language from the rule of signified spirituality or, on the other hand, convincingly to validate his own faith in a universe of metaphoric ideals. Hawthorne gradually reveals the sterility of the sentimental rule, which unfailingly inscribed the law of incarnation, referred the status of all texts toward presence, and enforced a textual metaphysics upon a consciousness that had lost its faith in presence. But though he makes his struggle clear, he could not relinquish the noumenal language which in fact he shared with Mrs. Stowe and the school of domestic sentiment.

In his earliest works, for example—*Twice-Told Tales* (1837) and *Mosses from an Old Manse* (1846)—signs which struggle to balance two orders, and attempt to transform one into the other, are especially evident in texts associated to desire. The marble monument bespoke by "an elderly lady . . . for her first-love . . . had given an ideality to her mind," Hawthorne tells us in "Chippings with a Chisel"; it had "kept her purer and less earthly than she would otherwise have been, by drawing a portion of her sympathies apart from earth."[13] In "The Prophetic Pictures," the portrait art which represents two lovers is (the painter muses) "the image of the Creator's own. The innumerable forms, that wander in nothingness, start into being at thy beck. . . . Thou recallest them to their old scenes, and givest their gray shadows the lustre of a better life, at once earthly and immortal" (IX.179). Here as always Hawthorne conflates the Actual and the Ideal to show that the order of the Ideal, of that which is signified, inheres in and dominates his signs of the sign—monuments, portraits, the metaphoric doublings and redoublings so important in his texts—as a voice or an image or a rune insisting that the sign's business is to transform phenomena into "magic . . . from the caverns of the soul" (IX.179), which the artist, as much a medium as his art, makes "by a power indefinable even to himself" (IX.175).

But even in this earliest work Hawthorne's typical use of signs reveals, together with the tendency to transform and spiritualize, a countertendency to which he is always responsive. No doubt this spiritualizing desire is modeled on Hawthorne's love for his wife, what Edgar Dryden has called his sense of "an incarnating act that frees rather than imprisons."[14] Hawthorne's lovers seek consolation in patterns; their desire helps them escape the uneasy depths that threaten to ruin the unity of his world. But Hawthorne always makes us aware that desire's escape is arbitrary. As Dryden points out, "The world of lovers . . . like the realm of romance, is one that

13. William Charvat, Roy Harvey Pearce, and Claude Simpson (eds.), *The Centenary Edition of the Works of Nathaniel Hawthorne* (16 vols. to date; Columbus, 1962–   ), IX, 410. Subsequent references will be given parenthetically in the text.

14. Edgar A. Dryden, *Nathaniel Hawthorne: The Poetics of Enchantment* (Ithaca, 1977), 84. Subsequent references will be given parenthetically in the text.

exists on the margin of the ordinary one, an artificial realm . . . a momentary one" (88). This is true, in fact, throughout Hawthorne; like the resolution of signs, all desire is momentary, and "the nature of the relationship between the Edenic, timeless world of the lovers and the wholly material one that exists on its boundaries remains in the form of an unanswered question" (92). Hawthorne always feels, even in the midst of transcendent love, a limitation which his erotic themes cannot escape, and he fears that his signs must fall short of their attempt to incarnate this structure. Yet he described his own *Twice-Told Tales* by saying, "Instead of passion, there is sentiment; and, even in what purport to be pictures of actual life, we have allegory. . . . The book . . . is apt to look exceedingly like a volume of blank pages" (IX.5). Henry James agreed; "Hawthorne, in his metaphysical moods" (James says) "is nothing if not allegorical, and allegory, to my sense, is quite one of the lighter exercises of the imagination."[15]

Indeed. But even F. O. Matthiessen admits that Hawthorne "failed to maintain a tenacious hold on the surfaces from which the realistic novelist draws his sustenance" and that his love of allegory became a problem.[16] Feidelson has also noted this, and concluded that Hawthorne is "not sure of his own stand," that he was split between the symbol, which "transcended analytic thought" but led away from a traditional paradigm into "disorder," and the more rational mode of allegory, which "depended on a conventional order whose point of arrangement was easily defined."[17] His symbolism was more true to his intelligence, no doubt; certainly his irony was; these acknowledge a freeplay of signs whose value comes not from their place in a metaphoric pattern but from their

15. Henry James, *Hawthorne* (Ithaca, 1956), 49. Subsequent references will be given parenthetically in the text.

16. F. O. Matthiessen, *American Renaissance: Art and Expression in the Age of Emerson and Whitman* (New York, 1941), 241.

17. Charles Feidelson, *Symbolism and American Literature* (Chicago, 1953), 14, 15. The question of Hawthorne's allegory has been vexed from the beginning. See for example John E. Becker, *Hawthorne's Historical Allegory: An Examination of the American Conscience* (Port Washington, N.Y., 1971); James K. Folsom, *Man's Accidents and God's Purposes: Multiplicity in Hawthorne's Fiction* (New Haven, 1963); and Don Parry Norford, "Rappaccini's Garden of Allegory," *American Literature*, L (1978), 167–86. But there are many more.

capacity to search, combine, and associate outside of the incarnational law—a scandalous undertaking; "symbolism leads to an inconclusive luxuriance of meaning, while allegory imposes the pat moral and the simplified character."[18] Symbolism allowed Hawthorne an ephemeral and nervous play, an agitated openness that marks a reassessment of the sign's balance. This begins an oscillation away from the emphatic vision of romantic metaphor, toward the privilege of "the desire for something else—of metonymy."[19] Symbolism brings the text back toward plurality, even at the risk— for Hawthorne especially—of fragmentation; where allegory, the most absolute form of metaphor, enforces a preference for monolithic abstractions, an understanding unified under a master law of signs. Allegory puts the sign at rest; symbolism keeps it open.

For Hawthorne, the allegorical enterprise is ultimately a movement toward something conceived both as universal and immutable. This is suggested by a passage from "Foot-prints on the Sea-shore" (in *Twice-Told Tales*), which opposes the artist's freedom to express aspects of his desire on a marginal place to an allegorized "Ocean," a portentous and vaguely theological activity in whose "unchanging voice" the "ages find utterance . . . and warn the listener to withdraw his interest from mortal vicissitudes, and let the infinite idea of eternity pervade his soul" (IX.460). Here we might well recall Lacan's observation that "desire begins to take shape in the margin in which demand becomes separated from need"—that margin which is the opening of a primal, steadfast distinction, a process of differentiation between what may and what may not be deferred.[20] For Lacan, the margin is a hypothetical place where sexual instincts are confronted by another human imperative, the need for a sustaining authority: the child's sexuality forgoes the parent, whose own sexuality, set aside by a prohibition, is thus lost and then sought elsewhere as a compensation; and this initiates all human desire, which always conforms to this structure.

Hawthorne's margin is less explicitly sexual, though it is clearly a

18. Feidelson, *Symbolism and American Literature*, 15.

19. Jacques Lacan, "The Agency of the letter in the unconscious or reason since Freud, in his *Ecrits*, trans. Alan Sheridan (New York, 1977), 167.

20. *Ibid.*, 311.

place where the erotic imagination tries to work free of an engulfing law by entering the play of signs. On his margin the name and
signs motivated by desire are briefly enfranchised. Hawthorne finds
he is enabled to fulfill a need: the margin allows him, he says, "to
think my own thoughts, and feel my own emotions, and possess
my individuality unviolated" (IX.461):

> This extensive beach affords room for pleasant pastime. With your staff,
> you may write verses—love-verses, if they please you best—and consecrate
> them with a woman's name. Here, too, may be inscribed thoughts, feelings,
> desires, warm outgushings from the heart's secret places, which you would
> not pour upon the sand without the certainty that, almost ere the sky has
> looked upon them, the sea will wash them out. . . . Now . . . draw huge
> faces—huge as that of the Sphynx on Egyptian sands. . . . Child's play be-
> comes magnificent on so grand a scale. But, after all, the most fascinating
> employment is simply to write your name in the sand. Draw the letters gi-
> gantic, so that two strides may barely measure them, and three for the long
> strokes! Cut deep, that the record may be permanent! . . . Is it accom-
> plished? Return, then, in an hour or two, and seek for this mighty record of
> a name. The sea will have swept over it, even as time rolls its effacing waves
> over the names of statesmen, and warriors, and poets. (IX.454–55)

This is Hawthorne's marginal text—a projection of the law of
signs which marks literature (as Geoffrey Hartman has said) with
"its excess over any assigned meaning, or, put more generally, the
strength of the signifier vis-à-vis a signified (the 'meaning') that
tries to enclose it."[21] On the "wet margin" (IX.452) where he
chooses to situate his text Hawthorne may phallically inscribe his
secrets (love, his name) and parenthesize them between "Ocean,"
the unthinking power that seems the deepest remove from human
intention or pleasure, and a society which he represents as distant
and mocking. The marginal text becomes a place of desire and language where the imagination is free of guilt and social demands, yet
never out of their sight, and where the illusion of "individuality unviolated" may declare itself.

It is helpful to set this passage next to Derrida's interrogation of
the textual margin. Derrida considers "all these boundaries that

21. Geoffrey Hartman, Preface to Harold Bloom, Jacques Derrida, Geoffrey Hartman, and J. Hillis Miller, *Deconstruction and Criticism* (New York, 1979), vii.

form the running border of what used to be called a text, of what we once thought this word would identify, i.e., the supposed end and beginning of a work, the unity of a corpus, the title, the margins, the signature, the referential realm outside the frame, and so forth."[22] What Derrida says happens to this traditional notion of the text has only begun to take place for Hawthorne—"a sort of overrun [debordement] that spoils all these boundaries and divisions" (83) and frees language to accept a pluralizing motive that has not yet been saturated by a single meaning, by an institutional identity of the signified; so that for Derrida the text "overruns all the limits assigned to it so far" (84). Derrida sees textuality as an engulfment of reality by inscriptions moving out through the margin that seems to make the text distinct from other semiotic systems. He wants to insist that the margin is not the place of differentiation between an enchanted order of writing and a larger, less coherent and alien scene which the text transcends, but rather that writing and all other conceptual systems are endlessly intertextual and mutually referential, all equally signifiers of one another's activity—fragments of an infinite but closed field, the idea of whose unity in some "elsewhere" only suppresses the freeplay and structurality of its components. For Derrida, whose sense of the sign here precisely opposes Hawthorne's, the energy of the signifier validates desire, the longing for what is lost, by constituting its own priority over a mystified ideal of unity. But for Hawthorne, writing a hundred and fifty years ago, it is the allegorical power of the signified which encroaches on the marginal place and overruns the text. The structure is the same, the results different.

This immense pressure of the signified, the demand for absolute homogeneity of meaning, overwhelms Hawthorne's free inscription of a signature. Nothing is more vulnerable than the text he figures as marginal, or more conflicted—the oceanic, simplifying force is inescapably a part of his textual scene; it typically makes its obliterating power felt there; it annexes the signifier's marginal place; it is a power which defines the margin of our freedom and in-fringes to determine it.

---

22. Jacques Derrida, "Living on—Border Lines," in Bloom et al., Deconstruction and Criticism, 83. Subsequent references will be given parenthetically in the text.

The mode which only begins to develop here in "Foot-prints on the Sea-shore," in this ephemeral gesture of independence from traditional signs, will come to realize itself later on in Derrida's theoretical model, "a 'text' that is henceforth no longer a finished corpus of writing, some content enclosed in a book or its margins, but a differential network, a fabric of traces referring endlessly to . . . other differential traces. Thus the text overruns all the limits assigned to it so far (not submerging or drowning them in an undifferentiated homogeneity, but rather making them more complex)" (84). This in fact will happen in our national literature, thanks to Melville's scandalous disruption of the sentimental paradigm and romantic metaphor. Unlike Hawthorne, who capitulates to the pure allegory of the signified, Melville prepares the way for a new mode of signs.

Hawthorne's tale, then, shows one power of the sign effacing the other. A theological figure, Ocean's voice, cancels the truancy of desire. Thinking of this effacement in a more general way, we might be reminded of the loving struggle between Clara Wieland and her brother, which eclipses knowing for both (one is mystified and the other deluded by the division of signifiers from the signified), or of the contrast of Cooper's Cora and Alice Munro: Alice swoons whenever her party enters the forest, and Cora is equally incompetent in the polite circles of stockade or city. Each of these pairs, like so many other equally well known American doublets, constitutes a marginal field of difference, a frontier where texts accept one order or the other—allegory or symbolism, civilization or wilderness, rule or freedom from rule. Perhaps it is the geographical peculiarity of the American experience—wilderness encountered by history, and after the invention of printing—that seems to make the configuration a special signature for American letters. In any case it is the structure of these differences, and no simple thematic opposition, that is important, a structure whose energies are often suggested by erotic desire or blood relationship, and sometimes by the conflation of these themes, as in Melville or Faulkner or James's *The Golden Bowl*.

Say it is a problem of Hawthorne's "sexual cowardice," uneasiness, or guilt caused by "furtive erotic gratification" which unsettles his expression of desire at a profound level—as Frederick Crews concludes, a "dynamics of repression and expression" which makes his use of metaphor, and of literary signs generally, so vexed here and throughout his career.[23] Whatever its source, the disturbance of the structure of signs is perfectly representative of romantic signification. Thomas McFarland has recently discussed "the disparactive triad" of "incompleteness, fragmentation, and ruin," problems which "permeate the human situation," and find insistent expression in the works of Coleridge and Wordsworth, whose opera are, McFarland shows, "famously incomplete," "torn and broken." The serenity of order is certainly a part of romantic textuality too, but it is impossible to think of romanticism without being made to realize, as McFarland urges, that "the phenomenology of the fragmentary is the phenomenology of human awareness."[24] The romantic privilege of metaphor noted by Jakobson, that is to say, extends from the transparent efficiency of metaphoric signs to a typical interest in their problematic and fragmented form which is, indeed, more characteristic.

Probably then one could divide romantic writers into those whose repression conventionalized desire and those whose imagination and language admitted otherwise repressed material as a subject. The fact of the division, and of the difficulty of making literary signs and texts out of opposing energies, would remain as their chief obsession. This is as true of Emerson and Mrs. Stowe as of Melville and Hawthorne: any signs brought consciously or unconsciously before the romantic imagination are understood in terms of their metaphoric doubleness, though in one version the metaphoricity of signs leads to transcendence and in the other to the questions and problems of a discontinuous reality. But however one chooses to view American romanticism, it must take shape as the record of attitudes toward an inherited metaphoric structure.

That it was an increasingly difficult and unsatisfying structure for Hawthorne begins to be clear in *Mosses from an Old Manse*. The sketch which introduces that volume, "The Old Manse," con-

23. Frederick Crews, *The Sins of the Fathers* (New York, 1966), 162, 163, 257.

24. Thomas McFarland, *Romanticism and the Forms of Ruin: Wordsworth, Coleridge, and Modalities of Fragmentation* (Princeton, 1981), 5, 6, 3. *Disparactive* is McFarland's coinage.

cerns itself not only with the image of a house which "had not quite the aspect of belonging to the material world" (X.3), but with the constant pressure of the theme and question of succession, which does as much to break the history of the house into fragments as it does to supply "objects made by men of other generations which still retain something of the human touch that created them." It is the river's flow that allows Hawthorne most freely to meditate on the relations of the soul (X.21ff). In writing of the Manse—which is surely an allusion to our imaginative tradition—he evokes the "succession of holy occupants [who] bequeath each an inheritance of sanctity to pervade the house and hover over it, as with an atmosphere" (X.4), including Emerson, who wrote *Nature* here (X.5). But then he sketches the accumulation of texts "that each generation has left behind it, from a period before the Revolution" (X.16). Some of these contain "marginal" comments which are "illegible," and they include a "vast folio" collection that is "too corpulent a body . . . to comprehend the spiritual element of religion" (X.18). These are texts in decay, counterpointing the rhythm of nature which in a parallel series of anecdotes carries on a sequence ending in the harvest of "real and tangible existences" (X.15) made possible by "the last clergyman," who planted seeds "in the pure and unselfish hope of benefitting his successors" (X.11). Unlike the "infinite generosity and exhaustless bounty" (X.13) of "wild nature . . . humanized" (X.12), which briefly refreshes the symbolic imagination and leads it to the transcendent image of the river (X.22), the legacy of old texts fails to sustain: "what was good and nourishing food for the spirits of one generation, affords no sustenance for the next" (X.19), Hawthorne says: "of this whole dusty heap of literature, I tossed aside all the sacred part" (X.20).

This emphasis on historical succession culminates in a definition of Hawthorne's place in the sequential habitation of the Manse—as a newlywed writer, not a clergyman, who substitutes his own desire for the burden of history and his own literary enchantments for the "dead trumpery" (X.19) of the attic library which is the legacy of the house. If he feels shadowed by his predecessors, as Crews suggests (31), he nonetheless understands clearly that their weight is a dead one, and he is at some pains to develop this evaluation at length as an introductory theme to his own collection of sketches, tales, and homilies about the American scene, a place whose signs require renewal since "the works of man's intellect decay like those of his hands" (X.19). The scene of "The Old Manse" is constituted by a difference between the ironic disparaction of myth into history and historical moments, and the vitalizing alternative of a truly spiritual nature, the river which recasts dead history as living myth and opposes barren textuality to a regenerating sign outside the Manse. The river is a "placid margin" (X.10) idealizing objects (and their reflections as well), moving through history as a reassuring source of inspiration.

In a wider sense the inspiration fails, however, since as Hawthorne reports, his residence in the Manse produces "no profound treatise of ethics—no philosophical history—no novel, even, that could stand, unsupported, on its edges" (X.34), that is, in the marginal place of freedom. He says much the same thing in "The Custom-House," where he recalls his eviction from the Manse after conceding that "a better book than I shall ever write was there," and goes on to express the hope that "at some future day, it may be, I shall remember a few scattered fragments and broken paragraphs, and write them down, and find the letters turn to gold upon the page" (I.37). The imagery reappears to mark the failure of *The Marble Faun,* and of textuality and writing, ten years after *The Scarlet Letter.* Here in *Mosses from an Old Manse* it is partially rationalized by a series of "discordant renovations" ordered by "the owner of the old house." These drive Hawthorne out in dismay: "The hand that renovates is always more sacrilegious than that which destroys" (X.33). What is sacrilegiously renovated by the house's owner, however, is not so much the Manse as what Hawthorne has made of it in his text: the scene of his own guilty renovation, which begins to clear away the obsolete rubbish of orthodox signs, refocus on the green world, and, against the weight of traditional resistance, commence the new and idiosyncratic literary mode expressed by the influence of Ellery Channing (X.21–26). But something intervenes, something always intervenes, as Ocean does in the earlier tale, to break off the enterprise conceived as a freedom to inscribe his own signature on the margin, the sign of his radical new vision, self-originated, "cut deep, that the record may be permanent!"

Throughout Hawthorne's career something invariably blocked his displacement of orthodox signs by new ones. Something intervened, something always intervened. James says of Hawthorne that "the imagination was profane, but the temper was not degenerate," a thing he would not have said of Melville, and perhaps this is it—Hawthorne had "no general views that were in the least uncomfortable"; what we see in his Diaries is "the exhibition of an unperplexed intellect" (22), and some aspiration or repression kept him from the realization of how thorough the revolution of the sign really needed to be.

Well, perhaps we need not go so far on James's road. Still one sees again and again that the creation of a brilliantly successful sign for desire, for instance Drowne's sculpted figurehead, which mediates real and ideal so well "that people knew not whether to suppose the magic wood etheralized into a spirit, or warmed and softened into an actual woman" (X.317), calls forth an answering, clumsy signature by the same hand, a sign in the opposing conservative mode. Drowne reverts to "the mechanical carver" (X.320) of inferior figures, and Hawthorne explains this by supposing "that in every human spirit there is imagination, sensibility, creative power, genius, which, according to circumstances, may either be developed in this world, or shrouded in a mask of dullness until another state of being' (X.319–20). A mysterious relationship between two orders of reality is expressed on this margin of desire, as we might hope the place of new signs; but generally we find that this new sign for art, created against the hostility of reactionary criticism, breaks under the rule of a strength which tends to be merely powerful, and often to lack intelligence. The rule may be signified as Drowne's wooden medium, an allegorical Ocean, or the blacksmith's sly son in "The Artist of the Beautiful," heir of a "hard, brute force that darkens and confuses the spiritual element" (X.454), whose "densest substance" (X.469) unthinkingly opposes "the spiritualization of matter" (X.459) and reduces Owen Warland's symbolic butterfly to "a small heap of glittering fragments, whence the Mystery of Beauty had fled forever" (X.475).[25]

This pattern of oppositions will surely be no surprise to readers of Hawthorne. What I want to insist on is the possibility that it projects a central and structural dilemma, that of reshaping literary signs, which always consist not only of the energy of an imagination but also of the immense pressure of inherited forms, of ideas become sedimented, knowledge become inert. These two imperatives work against one another to engender a field of possibilities, one that finally remains unrealized by Hawthorne: each of his texts reenacts the struggle of its predecessors without ever becoming free of it.

One could easily enough identify a number of places in the novels which reproduce this central problem of structure. One well-known example is the episode in Chapter 19 of *The Scarlet Letter*, "The Child at the Brook-side," in which Pearl, her image doubled by reflections in the water, standing across a bordering stream from her parents but situated with them on the frontier between civilization and wilderness, next to the "ruined wall" of the human soul (I.200–201), serves as "the living hieroglyphic, in which was revealed the secret they so darkly sought to hide . . . the oneness of their being . . . the material union, and the spiritual idea, in whom they met, and were to dwell immortally together" (I.207). Oppositions and margins multiply here to call attention to new possibilities for literary language. The place is intermediate and divisive in any number of ways—for Hester it is a "moral wilderness" as well, an estrangement from which she looks back at "human institutions" (I.199); it puts on the one hand the "wild, heathen Nature of the forest, never subjugated by human law, nor illumined by higher truth" (I.203), and on the other not only civilization but Dimmesdale, "the head of the social system . . . trammelled by its regulations, its principles, and even its prejudices. . . . the framework of his order inevitably hemmed him in" (I.200).

In terms of the sign's structure, this episode takes place at a cru-

25. For a discussion of Hawthorne's manipulation of the "general antithesis of ideal and material" (72) in "The Artist of the Beautiful," see Richard Harter Fogle, *Hawthorne's Fiction: The Light and the Dark* (Norman, 1952), 70–90.

cial place or moment: at the division between sign, the "cut in discourse . . . which acts as a bar between the signifier and the signified."[26] This border, frontier, or point of absolute limit, both joining and division, is the place in the equation of the sign where signifier and signified, the clarity of the fragment and the power of unity, agree upon the form which will express their relationship. Each insists upon a role and concedes one. Neither power can go forward; neither can constitute meaning in isolation; each has reached its limit, and the two opposites must negotiate an agreement, an agreement whose tangible form is the sign itself. Eric Sundquist points out that "Hawthorne's interest in the 'threshold' often lies in the pursuit of a bloody footstep that marks the boundary between the hypothetical Eden and the speculative world of transgression."[27] This draws attention, one might say, to the scandalous promise of limits, to the margin on the edge of law where the instinct of desire accomplishes one of two things: if it escapes it initiates the freedom which reoriginates symbolicity; if ruled it accepts traditional laws of expression, which for Hawthorne were always found in the matrix of the soul and the literature of the hearth, powers which tend to suppress or transform desire.

If the result is freedom from rule, one gains the scandal that springs the rhythm of culture out of its meter. This violation forces law's reinscription under fresh circumstances; and a new order of signification, without reference to sedimented values, becomes possible. Thus the invention of culture may be repeated in every signifying act, at the end of each signifying chain—the structure of the sign encodes that original event and ensures the possibility of its repetition; the sign conserves not only order but, thanks to the margin which can also be a ruined wall, the possibility of scandal as well.

For Hawthorne to allow the open acceptance of Hester and Pearl by Dimmesdale would be scandalous in this sense. In such a decision desire would ratify itself; it would break the power of the old

26. Lacan, "The subversion of the subject and the dialectic of desire in the Freudian unconscious," *Ecrits*, 299.

27. See Eric J. Sundquist, *Home as Found: Authority and Genealogy in Nineteenth-Century American Literature* (Baltimore, 1979), 124.

law to determine motive and action; it would disclose the freedom of desire to predicate itself outside the confinement of law, acknowledging instinct and privileging it. An acknowledgment like this, in which desire is celebrated rather than punished, would oppose the overdetermined sign of Salem, the "wooden edifice, the door of which was heavily timbered with oak, and studded with iron spikes" (I.47). Desire would be admitted to discourse, would begin discourse as new. Then it would be possible to set Anne Hutchinson's rose, "the deep heart of Nature" which can "pity and be kind" (I.48) and which magically appears at the place of birth into confinement, above the image which is privileged instead: the town-beadle, who "like a black shadow emerging into the sunshine . . . prefigured and represented in his aspect the whole dismal severity of the Puritanic code of law" (I.52).

But Hawthorne's texts always draw back before the promise that culture's "contrivance of wood and iron" (I.55) could be thrown down by a violation. Dimmesdale's hesitation seconds Hawthorne's reluctance to privilege the brilliant, moving power of Hester's instinct over the repression of an institutional signified. And if Dimmesdale points to Hawthorne's reluctance, Pearl more broadly suggests Hawthorne's ambivalence. The anxiety of her energy is partly an understanding that his world cannot allow such an original identity as hers to assume authority. She is Hawthorne's conflicted image of power on the margin of desire, the sign of his inability to reconstitute signs as something new. If Hawthorne endows her with a future, if she becomes the heiress of a renovated world (the hasty illusion of such promise is characteristic of his fiction), it is not as a fully developed subject. She is above all a muted and ambiguous value, alienated from the harsh problems of her tale and therefore from the scene of its meaning (this seems to be the point), a generic link to the fairy tale: mechanically she provides a difficult text with a happy but unconvincing ending. She does not found a new understanding, because Hawthorne could not give scandal its voice, or allow it depth or promise of renewal, or efface the institution of the sign so as to place himself (or Dimmesdale) at the beginning as a father of new meanings. Instead he allows the order of institutions to overshadow desire's strength to elide and restructure law.[28]

Hawthorne grants this same force to the institutions represented in *The House of the Seven Gables* (1851) and *The Blithedale Romance* (1852), both of which absorb symbolic violations into the domestic system and hedge the danger of scandal by stating it as a moral ambiguity. This was also the case in "The Old Manse," where, Hawthorne says, it seems finally to him "that all the artifice and conventionalism of life was but an impalpable thinness upon [the river's] surface, and that the depth below was none the worse for it. . . . I prayed that the upper influences might long protect the institutions that had grown out of the heart of mankind" (X.25–26).

But scandal is a necessary event in the history of structure. Hawthorne comes closest to admitting this in *The Marble Faun* (1860), a text in which he almost manages to liberate the sign from the dominance of the signified. He sets this novel in Rome, the ruin of the type of all cities, "a shapeless confusion of modern edifices, piled rudely up with ancient brick and stone, and over the domes of Christian churches, built on the old pavements of heathen temples, and supported by the very pillars that once upheld them" (IV.6). Of all Hawthorne's signs for culture, such as the oak and iron door of the Salem jail or the "rusty wooden house" (II.5) of the Pyncheons, this "cultural desuetude" (Daniel Hoffman calls it) is the richest and the closest to degeneration.[29] Too, the novel opens with the image of "the Dying Gladiator, just sinking into his death swoon," focusing the other "famous productions of antique sculpture . . . still shining in the undiminished majesty and beauty of their ideal life," but nonetheless "yellow with time, and perhaps corroded" (IV.5). The icons that contend for the mastery of Hawthorne's uni-

28. For a good reading of this episode, see Michael Davitt Bell, *Hawthorne and the Historical Romance of New England* (Princeton, 1971), 186–88. See also the excellent discussion of the difference between the lost realm of natural innocence and the complexities of a fallen culture in Edgar A. Dryden's "The Limits of Romance: A Reading of *The Marble Faun*," in Kenneth H. Baldwin and David N. Kirby (eds.), *Individual and Community: Variations on a Theme in American Fiction* (Durham, 1975), 17–48.

29. Daniel G. Hoffman, *Form and Fable in American Fiction* (New York, 1961), 105.

verse, images of art's order and culture's, now indicate deterioration more than strength. They are surrendering to death. Dryden
speaks of "the failure of mediated relations" in *The Marble Faun,* a
"reflexiveness" that "has the effect of creating a realm which has no
apparent beginning outside itself but seems made of words whose
meaning depends not on some reality which lies behind them but
on other words."[30] Indeed culture seems as enervated as art, and
law as faded as the past, in this world where desire is represented as
the reenactment of a myth, or recapitulates a literary convention,
but in either case repeats rather than originates. Still, more than
ever before Hawthorne has set his imagination a promising scene
for renovating the obsolete structure of meaning.

In other words scandal brings us close to the nucleus of signs in
this text, which dwells on the failure and death of signification and
which begins to find a motif whose implication (it is nothing less
than the end of metaphor), once it has been introduced into the
plot, seems inescapable. This is the threat of incest, extremest and
most original form of desire. Incest is the uncombining act of which
all the other failures of culture's order are only symptoms. It is
the epitome of scandal; but having suggested it Hawthorne draws
back, even amid his deployment of these ruins, and refuses to imagine the result of using an incestuous desire to question the forms of
meaning. But he does at least portray the symptoms of this crisis of
structure, and reveals, by his familiar strategy of returning to the
discourse of law, the anomie of the signified, whose obsolescence is
now unquestionable.

The first suggestion of incest appears in Chapter 7, "Beatrice,"
where Miriam interprets Hilda's copy of Guido's *Beatrice Cenci.*
Hitherto only one copy has been made, the details of the painting
brought away "piece-meal" (IV.65), since its reproduction is, fit-
tingly enough, forbidden. Of course the repetition of incest is
barred. The subject of the portrait, Hilda says, "knows that her
sorrow is so strange, and so immense, that she ought to be solitary
forever, both for the world's sake and her own" (IV.65). Beatrice,
Hilda innocently believes, is a "fallen angel, fallen, and yet sinless"

30. Dryden, *The Poetics of Enchantment,* 36, 38–39.

(IV.66), and her remark provokes Miriam to open the question of incestuous guilt, to insist on the alternatives of sorrow and sin: does not Beatrice's look suggest "something evil . . . never to be forgiven"? she asks. And Hilda immediately concurs—she had forgotten the parricide and incest which predicate the suffering: "Yes, yes; it was terrible guilt, an inexpiable crime. . . . Her doom is just" (IV.66).

Obviously Miriam has repeated the violation of Beatrice Cenci in some way. We never see or hear of the event directly; its nature is oblique and evasive; the *raisonneur,* Kenyon, absorbs the burden of knowledge for us in a private conversation with Miriam in which she "spoke of her own life, and told facts that threw a gleam of light over many things" (IV.429):

> She revealed a name, at which her auditor started, and grew pale; for it was one, that, only a few years before, had been familiar to the world, in connection with a mysterious and terrible event. . . .
> . . . the frightful and mysterious circumstances of which will recur to many minds, but of which few or none can have found for themselves a satisfactory explanation. (IV.430, 431)

Mysterious or not, the association with Beatrice Cenci; Miriam's shadowy follower, who is oddly referred to as "Father"; and the language describing their relationship (they are linked "by a bond equally torturing to each . . . forged in some such unhallowed furnace as is only kindled by evil passions and fed by evil deeds" [73])—all clarify what must be taken as an unspeakable violation, one which ultimately draws the innocents Donatello and Hilda, and to some extent the skeptical Kenyon, and therefore the structural patterns as well as the setting of the fictive world, into the circle of textual contamination.

The influence of Melville's thematics of incest in *Pierre* also suggests that it is the threat of incest—and of the disclosure of incest—which causes Donatello to murder Miriam's sinister companion. But the complex motive of the crime is immediately evaded by something more recuperative, the allegory of the Fortunate Fall. This reenactment of the Fall serves as a defense against the prior and more mysterious transgression that it screens. Thus a powerful old order defends against the scandalization of its laws by restating the ultimate crime as something subordinate to itself, something which is clearly under law. But the allegory growing out of Hawthorne's insertion of this renovated myth cannot adequately explain the original violation which brings his fictive world into ruins. It does allow Kenyon to propose two entirely different and contradictory explanations of reality to Hilda: innocence is wholly lost to man; or crime is the agency of our moral and intellectual awakening (IV.459–60). But neither of these is sufficient. The first, Hilda cannot accept; the second "annuls and obliterates whatever precepts of Heaven are written deepest within us" (IV.460). The text and its readers are therefore left between options, in the half-world of possibility, "a sort of poetic or fairy precinct" (IV.3), which was, at the beginning of Hawthorne's career, the place where art mediated differences, but which is now a margin of despair and death: "Thus, between two countries, we have none at all, or only that little space of either, in which we finally lay down our discontented bones" (IV.461).

The margin of signs has become the grave of meaning. It is no wonder, then, that art seems to have lost its consecration. Even Hilda is so affected by Miriam's ramified crime that her mystically sympathetic response to painting fails. Sculpture is scandalized as well, its form fragmented in an episode which ties the text's plurality of reference—culture, law, art, writing, desire—to a single broken image, one which signals the loss of spiritual reality in Hawthorne's universe. If there is any key to understanding in this text, whose fragmentation sometimes seems to be its chief meaning, perhaps it is here. Kenyon, sitting alone in the slanting sunshine, sees at his feet what he first takes to be "a shapeless fragment of stone" (IV.422). To relieve an "anxious tedium" he excavates a "figure of marble . . . earth-stained . . . slightly corroded . . . [but] wonderfully delicate and beautiful." The head is gone, both arms are broken at the elbow; but Kenyon discovers first one hand, then the other, and "Placing these limbs in what the nice adjustment of the fractures proved to be their true position, the poor, fragmentary woman forthwith showed that she retained her modest instincts. . . . these long-buried hands immediately disposed themselves in the manner that nature prompts, as the antique artist knew, and as all the world has seen, in the Venus de'Medici." At once Kenyon sees a meaning in the reconstructed sign: "'I seek for Hilda, and find a marble woman! Is the omen good or ill?'" (IV.423).

Gradually something appears to be taking shape from the debris of culture in this Roman field of ruin. Nowhere else in the novel, we should bear in mind, does fragmentation allow us to recombine the original shape of things. No other litter of fragments thus permits reassembly; but here, when Kenyon lifts another "small, round block of stone" and places it on the neck of his discovery,

> the effect was magical. It immediately lighted up and vivified the whole figure, endowing it with personality, soul, and intelligence. The beautiful Idea at once asserted its immortality, and converted that heap of forlorn fragments into a whole, as perfect to the mind, if not to the eye, as when the new marble gleamed with snowy lustre. . . .
>
> It was either the prototype or a better repetition of the Venus of the Tribune . . . [but with a] far nobler and sweeter countenance. It is one of the few works of antique sculpture in which we recognize Womanhood, and that, moreover, without prejudice to its divinity. (IV.423–24)

What is being reassembled here? On the shattered stone body of woman is represented the regeneration of art, the form of an immortal ideal, the possibility of recollection and even of transcendence. The broken Venus is a kind of altar, and Kenyon a kind of priest. What takes place is an apotheosis: "The world was richer than yesterday, by something far more precious than gold. Forgotten beauty had come back, as beautiful as ever; a goddess had risen from her long slumber, and was a goddess still" (IV.424). Kenyon's discovery and arrangement recuperates the lost perfect form of an Ideal and reverses the direction along which scandal impels the order of fiction. This rubble of the sign miraculously recombines along the axis of metaphor; an entire order is predicated on the debris of these signifiers. Not just an ideal but the presence of ideality is suddenly resurrected and incarnated from this litter of fragments, the broken Venus which perfects the image of desire and restores it to man as innocent: an idealized value of desire was lost and is found—and "without prejudice to its divinity!"

But it was only briefly that Kenyon "exaggerated" the importance of his discovery: "In reality he found it difficult to fix his
mind upon the subject. . . . there was something dearer to him
than his art; and, by the greater strength of a human affection, the
divine statue seemed to fall asunder again, and become only a heap
of worthless fragments" (IV.424). Like "the sculptured scene on the
sarcophagus" (IV.89) and the celebration in the Borghese Gardens
(Chapter 10), dances which seem briefly to call back the Golden
Age, and like the myth of Adam's temptation and Fall, this idealized meaning is obscured by something which works against the
recuperation of lost ideals.

The dance, the broken Venus, the myth of the Fall—these three
figures (to which we might add the legend of Monte Beni recounted
in Chapter 26 and the Carnival in Chapters 47 and 48) are all ex-
pressions of a spontaneous desire which forgets, but then remem-
bers, the imposition of law. Like dance, whose movements always
risk a fall but then overcome it, these bring desire under meter, for-
malize it, subordinate it to the idea of limits. Thus do inclinations
and instincts come under the rule of signs. In a sense all these
myths represent not the release but the containment of an ecstatic,
primal desire which is older than law. They suggest a play of release
and control that imitates the difference and tension between satisfaction and deferral, the activity which governs all signification.
But none of Hawthorne's metaphors is sufficiently strong to countermand and control Miriam's absolute crime, not even the myth of
the Fall, which in any case is only the worse scandal of incest displaced onto dogma, or to resist the dissolving incest which leaves
the shadow of its question on all form.[31]

31. For a wholly rationalized interpretation of Miriam's mysterious crime, see Roy R.
Male, *Hawthorne's Tragic Vision* (New York, 1964), 168; for his reading of the motif of
the Fortunate Fall, 174–76. See also Hyatt H. Waggoner, *Hawthorne: A Critical Study*
(Rev. ed.; Cambridge, Mass., 1963): "All Rome, all history, made the crime inevitable,
and its spreading effects leave no one untouched, not even the spotless Hilda. This murder is no ordinary crime but a re-enactment of the archetypal fall" (211). For Waggoner
it *is* a fortunate fall (217). But *cf.* Leslie A. Fiedler, *Love and Death in the American
Novel* (New York, 1960): The "suggestions of immemorial inbreeding, joined with the
repeated allusions to Miriam's implication in 'one of the most dreadful and mysterious
events that have occurred within the present century' implies surely the sin of incest; but

But what then? Hawthorne returns not only to the familiar in-stitutions but to those dogmatic literary signs which are the cold trace of presence. He makes Kenyon give over his attempt to under-stand the mysteries of instinct and ecstasy, and plead for Hilda's help: "I have neither pole star above, nor light of cottage-windows here below, to bring me home. . . . Oh, Hilda, guide me home!" And Hilda is brought down from her Virgin's Tower "to be herself enshrined and worshipped as a household Saint, in the light of her husband's fireside," to occupy that little intermediate space "be-tween two countries"—America and Italy, or matter and spirit—where "we finally lay down our discontented bones" (IV.460–61).[32] Is this the exhaustion of bad faith? Or perhaps Hilda feels what Hawthorne once seems to have felt himself, "that icy Demon of Weariness who . . . possesses the magic that is the destruction of all other magic" (IV.336), even the magic that he sought at the beginning of his career, the "magic . . . from the caverns of the soul."

In "The New Adam and Eve" (a story in *Mosses from an Old Manse*) Hawthorne had spoken of the confinements of "the world's artificial system," and insisted "It is only through the medium of the imagination that we can loosen those iron fetters, which we call truth and reality" (X.247). He suggests toward the end of this tale that beginning culture over, after a "Day of Doom" (X.247) which extinguishes human life, will set the race free of inherited errors—if Eve can keep Adam from "the mysterious perils of the library," which would pass on to him our "whole heap of disastrous lore" (X.265). Then man's new literature, "when the progress of cen-turies shall create it, will be no interminable repeated echo of our own poetry, and reproduction of the images that were moulded by

Hawthorne is at once too genteel and too fond of playful mystification to speak out that dread word" (402). Frederick Crews suggests that we should draw our inference from what he rightly identifies as "the emotional starvation that ensues from a morbid dread of incest" and from the attitude shared by the characters that "all life is seen in a back-ward glance from the brink of nothingness" (*The Sins of the Fathers*, 183, 214).

32. See Fogle, *The Light and the Dark*, 191–92, 196–97; Waggoner, *Hawthorne*, 221; and Matthiessen, *American Renaissance*, 360. There is some agreement that the complexity of the text remains unresolved: its ambiguity, its ambivalence, and its charac-teristic unsteady reliance on the value of institutions are a problem.

our great fathers of song and fiction." Instead literary signs will represent something truly original, "a melody never yet heard on earth, and intellectual forms unbreathed by our conceptions" (X.266). The vision is brilliant, but Hawthorne was not the one to recommence. His texts fall somewhere between the institutions which determine interpretation and the scandal which demands it should falter and begin again.

What did Hawthorne mean in returning to the sentimental iconography of household saints and firesides? What did he escape in evading the fullest energy of violation? I have been urging, as the motive of Hawthorne's figuration, his place in a structure which dictates the form of his anxieties and ideas, even of his signs. This structure is shared, not idiosyncratic. What is idiosyncratic is the way in which different writers of fiction respond, thematically and figuratively, to the alternating pressures of the sign's structure—to festive dance, say, and to scandal. Mrs. Stowe uses signs to celebrate a system which Melville ruins. Hawthorne attempts to mediate these extremes. His fiction records an increasingly inadequate middle ground which in *The Marble Faun* becomes the grave; and his text is the monument above it. But for the clearest sense of what is implied at either end of the oscillation of the sign we should turn to *The Minister's Wooing* and to *Pierre*.

CHAPTER II

Harriet Beecher Stowe and the Structure of Desire

He shall be filled with the Holy Ghost, even from his mother's womb.

—Luke 1:15

He invented mother's hearts, and He certainly has the pattern in his own.

—Charles Edward Stowe

Theology defines maternity only as an impossible elsewhere, a sacred beyond, a vessel of divinity, a spiritual tie with the ineffable godhead, and transcendence's ultimate support—necessarily virginal and committed to assumption.

—Julia Kristeva

Begin by looking upward through my epigraphs: to maternity, to mothers' hearts, and thus—only thus—toward God. Your glance toward these pretexts replicates the movement that is my subject, the tendency of desire in sentimental fiction.[1] Once all texts had in mind a transparent language whose form was the visible graph of invisible meaning, and writing enfolded another value which it systematically expressed and with which it was coalescent: written discourse was not limited to the matrix of factual historical reality; "in its original form, when it was given to men by God himself, language was an absolutely certain and transparent sign for things, because it resembled them."[2]

1. There is a steadily growing critical literature on sentimental fiction in nineteenth-century America. The founding examination is Herbert Ross Brown's *The Sentimental Novel in America, 1789–1860* (New York, 1959). Perhaps the most influential of recent studies is Ann Douglas, *The Feminization of American Culture* (New York, 1977). An excellent summary of critical attitudes toward sentimental literature is offered in Mary Kelley's "The Sentimentalists: Promise and Betrayal in the Home," *Signs*, IV (1979), 434–46, and a good historical survey of the mode is Nina Baym, *Woman's Fiction: A Guide to Novels by and About Women in America, 1820–1870* (Ithaca, 1978).
2. Michel Foucault, *The Order of Things: An Archaeology of the Human Sciences*, trans. unacknowledged (New York, 1970), 36.

Subsequently and gradually language is demoted; it falls away from these original values, or so the myth of language goes, "and creates within its own space everything that will ensure a ludic denial of them (the scandalous, the ugly, the impossible)."[3] For Jonathan Edwards, Perry Miller argues, "the word, according to [Locke's] doctrine, becomes *detachable* from . . . sensation. It can be spoken separately by those who have forgotten the experience, by those who barely felt it, even by those who never had it and have no 'actual idea' of the experience at all. . . . if the impact of the experience grows dim, if the sensation subsides like a shadowy memory, the word . . . may be used *as though* the experience were still actual and so cease to be anything but a hollow sound." Any experience, any word, any aspect of the human condition at a distance from God, is thus broken, and drifts with every use, and every representation, farther away from presence, and carries men with it. So, Miller goes on, "From this state—which is original sin—they must be redeemed. The regenerate state thus becomes one with that living, pulsating state in which a word is vividly, fully identified with its sensation. As life is lived from day to day, the name imperceptibly takes the place of the sensation, and ultimately becomes the only object for the idea. By then the idea itself becomes a decaying phantasm and only verbal knowledge remains. To our horror we realize that we are lost among signs."[4]

The fall has been incorporated by this discourse, which comes to replicate man's alienation and his loss; and the challenge faced by Edwardsean language was the discovery of a style which could represent the restoration of spiritual life to the system of words. The shadow of the broken law fell on Edwards' style and enforced a severity that worked against the heart's movement. It was law and its logic that took precedence over the heart's affections, which had already led man to the fall. But in the fiction I am beginning to describe signs are meant to incorporate, to be filled with and to yield, an ideal version of the phenomenal real which works free of the law's vision of a depraved race, and restores human affections to

3. *Ibid.*, 300.
4. Perry Miller, "Jonathan Edwards on the Sense of the Heart," *Harvard Theological Review*, XLI (1948), 125, 126–27.

a central and effective role. It is helpful to understand this language through the trope of maternity, the theological maternity which is "an impossible elsewhere"[5]—a maternity which hedges the ludic denial, validates the heart, and rescues desire from its play and its scandal. Through desire, language is recuperated; and through language, the divine signature. Maternity reifies *ecstasis,* the soul's relocation outside the body. Thanks to maternity desire turns away from the fallen place of nature toward a genesis of spirit, and the natural body of woman, the Venus which Hawthorne failed to reassemble for us, transforms and is consecrated: desire as instinct is exchanged for desire as grace.[6] Nature is thereby redeemed as desire is celebrated and canceled in the same image: realized in nativity, neutralized in motherhood, because desire focused by the mother becomes impossible and moves elsewhere. The first law of culture, the prohibition against incest, ordains this. Desire is then an event in the preterite, repressed and already forgotten. Sentimental desire, like sentimental language, "contains its own inner principle of proliferation."[7] This is always apparent as the promise of nativity, sexuality outside desire and altogether apart from it—as "woman's nature . . . as the pure priestess of a domestic temple."[8]

So sentimental fiction opens to its readers with the reminder that they are separated, by a gaze filled with longing beyond satisfaction, from the mystical body that once abided them. In this fictional mode we follow, and are distinct from, a beginning that was formerly immediate: coexistent, simultaneous, identical, but now lost to us. But more importantly, the rules of this fiction develop the possibility of a natural return, through maternal intervention, to

5. Julia Kristeva, "Motherhood According to Giovanni Bellini," in her *Desire in Language: A Semiotic Approach to Literature and Art,* ed. Leon S. Roudiez, trans. Thomas Gora, Alice Jardine, and Leon S. Roudiez (New York, 1980), 237.

6. See Jane P. Tompkins, "Sentimental Power: *Uncle Tom's Cabin* and the Politics of Literary History," *Glyph 8* (1981), 79–102. The place of maternity in sentimental fiction is discussed at length by Tompkins (95–98). See also a fine earlier essay by Elizabeth Ammons, "Heroines in *Uncle Tom's Cabin*," *American Literature,* XLIX (1977), esp. 164–65, and Ann D. Wood, "The 'Scribbling Women' and Fanny Fern: Why Women Wrote," *American Quarterly,* XXIII (1971), 3–24.

7. Foucault, *The Order of Things,* 40.

8. Harriet Beecher Stowe, *The Minister's Wooing* (New York, 1859), 230. Subsequent references, abbreviated *MW,* will be given parenthetically in the text.

that absent unity. Maternal intervention becomes the matrix—*matrix* means maternal abode, the womb which (no longer) encloses us—at which we are gazing, and through which we may return to an original myth of infancy: *infans,* without speech, without need for language but replete with intention and understanding. Thus, Harriet Beecher Stowe writes, "doubts are resolved in the region of religious faith," where God "treats us as the mother does her 'infant crying in the dark'; He does not reason with our fears, or demonstrate their fallacy, but draws us silently to His bosom" (MW 425–26).

But this resolution can only begin with the gaze of desire: literally the longing for an absent or lost person or thing; for the matrix, the lost maternal context, with which we were formerly simultaneous and identical. Desire, the sense of absence or loss, seeks unity with an origin by making itself transcendent—surpassing and outside natural experience: the womb or matrix of being. "The blessedness of Mary," Mrs. Stowe once said, "was that she was the one human being who had the right of ownership and intimate oneness with the Beloved."[9] Like any mother of any son "she loves the father and herself united and made one in this young heir of life and hope" (284); and, Mrs. Stowe went on, since Christ was "the union of the divine nature with the nature of a pure woman . . . there was in Jesus more of the pure feminine element than in any other man. It was the feminine element exalted and taken in unity with identity" (RS 36).[10] In sentimental fiction, desire seeks simultaneity and identity with this sustaining body, this text of texts, which it always begins by observing as lost and which it returns to us as an icon.

In novels of domestic sentiment, then, erotic desire looks for and is quick to find an alibi, the "impossible elsewhere" of maternity that purifies desire and acquits the flesh. Maternity is an exonerat-

9. Harriet Beecher Stowe, *Religious Studies: Sketches and Poems* (Boston, 1896), 34. Subsequent references will be identified by the abbreviation RS and given parenthetically in the text.

10. See Ammons, "Heroines in *Uncle Tom's Cabin*," 164–65. In *The Feminization of American Culture,* Ann Douglas writes that Mrs. Stowe "triumphantly displayed the scene of man abject under feminine rule. She managed to analyze and mock the futilities inherent in the position of the liberal minister and the male sentimentalist; she recorded an enormous scorn for masculinity itself" (244). But this goes too far.

ing tabernacle for sexuality.[11] In T. S. Arthur's *The Maiden, Wife, and Mother* it seems appropriate for James Hartley to confess to his wife "No act is too tender for a mother. Her kiss upon my cheek, her warm embrace, are all felt now, and the older I grow the more holy seem the influences that surrounded me in childhood."[12] How easily the genial notion of mother translates into physical details, kiss, embrace, and then back into the spirituality of holy influence! And it is the logic of this influence to become definitive: "As you have been a good wife, you will be a good mother."[13] Anna Hartley "has performed the highest and holiest of offices—she has given birth to an immortal being." Soul begets soul; this is the inevitable displacement of desire by maternity. Arthur's narrator, the voice of the sentimental text, redefines the erotic life of woman: "Hereafter we must know [her] in the twofold character of wife and mother, for they are inextricably blended," and James Hartley puts it more strongly still: "Now that she held to him the twofold relation of a wife and mother," he muses, "his love was increased fourfold. He thought of her, and looked upon her, with increased tenderness."[14]

Her significance multiplies, the icon rises to become vertical and monumental and to orient social and domestic, not to say erotic, life. When mother can no longer be distinguished from wife, value doubles, quadruples, becomes immeasurable and imperative; we "must know" wife as mother. The relationship is metaphorical, even magical—transcendent: Anna Hartley "felt that she was indeed beginning a new life. Every hour her soul seemed to enlarge. . . . all was peace within—holy peace. There came a Sabbath rest of deep interior joy. . . . Body and spirit entered into this rest. She was the same, and not the same."[15]

Today we cannot fail to see this icon as the sign of "the feminine,

11. See Dorothy Berkson, "Millennial Politics and the Feminine Fiction of Harriet Beecher Stowe," in Elizabeth Ammons (ed.), *Critical Essays on Harriet Beecher Stowe* (Boston, 1980), 244–58, on the feminine idea of Christ and patriarchal religious values.

12. T. S. Arthur, *The Mother*, in his *The Maiden, Wife, and Mother* (Philadelphia, 1845–46). These three novels, each independently paginated, are bound as a single volume, but must be cited individually.

13. Arthur, *The Wife*, 159.

14. Arthur, *The Mother*, 158, 159.

15. *Ibid.*, 157.

verbal scarcity so prevalent in our culture"—the wife richly endowed, but only with sensibility and silence: "Women have nothing
but their heart" (*MW* 477). Here, we would say, woman is granted
a power that can only limit her. In the context of this fiction, however, she is intended to seem a prophetic voice. Language and the
maternal woman similarly enfold the reader's imagination and (his)
perception of values. They are both filled with presence; they incorporate "the sacred beyond"—each is fructified by "a spiritual tie
with the ineffable godhead": maternal mediation supplements and
finally replaces the institutional (which is to say masculine and paternal) authority of writing.[16] The "intellect, cold, is ever more
masculine than feminine" (Margaret Fuller said): "warmed by
emotion, it rushes toward mother-earth, and puts on the form of
beauty."[17] Mrs. Stowe agreed; she shared, as it were, the sentiment:
"If we consider that the Son of God, as to his human nature, was
made of a woman, it leads us to see that in matters of grace God sets
a special value on woman's nature and designs to put special honor
upon it" (*MW* 364). Thus in 1857, the year before *The Minister's
Wooing* commenced its serial publication in the *Atlantic,* Mrs.
Stowe's sister Catherine Beecher "expressed her mature views" by
dedicating *Common Sense Applied to Religion* not "'respectfully
to an honored and beloved Father,' but to 'the People, as the safest
and truest interpreters of the Bible, and TO WOMAN, as the heaven-
appointed educator of Mind.'"[18]

From this sentimental perspective the absolute maternity of signs
suppresses any nativity that is not iconic. Even Margaret Fuller
conceded that: "if it be true, as the legend says, that Humanity
withers through a fault committed by and a curse laid upon Woman,
through her pure child, or influence, shall the new Adam, the redemption, arise. Innocence is to be replaced by virtue, dependence
by a willing submission, in the heart of the Virgin-Mother of the
new race" (102). Here in the comparative radicalism of *The Dial*

16. Kristeva, "Motherhood According to Giovanni Bellini," 237.

17. Margaret Fuller, *Woman in the Nineteenth Century* (New York, 1971), 103. Subsequent references will be given parenthetically in the text.

18. Charles H. Foster, *The Rungless Ladder: Harriet Beecher Stowe and New
England Puritanism* (Durham, 1954), 96.

the social limitations of the metaphor become briefly evident: "Women are, indeed, the easy victims of priest-craft and delusion" (105) when sentimental enchantment flourishes; viewed so narrowly, women "are likely to be enslaved by an impassioned sensibility" (103). The contemporary fictional mode admits no irony, however. Women and language identically mediate different orders of reality; they draw together; they seem always to have drawn together, matter and spirit. Both language and woman provide incarnations that orient reality toward transcendence. Women are therefore the scene and the type of metaphor.

This power of feminized language is what supplements and refocuses the predominating Edwardsean idea of language. Mrs. Stowe says of the Seventy-second Psalm, for instance, that it "expands into language" and becomes "a great tide of imagery that belong[s] to nothing earthly" (RS 16). Indeed the tradition of her father held that all Scripture—every instance of it, according to his colleague Nathaniel Emmons—"bears the stamp of a divine signature, and carries its own internal evidence with it to the understandings, and consciences, and hearts of all, who have candidly and impartially considered it."[19] Language "bears . . . internal evidence"; the passage evokes a sense of pregnancy, which is, however, immediately identified as a paternal inscription on its form: the signature is stamped as on a coin. And "there is no difference between the visible marks God has stamped upon the surface of the earth, so that we may know its inner secrets, and the legible words that the Scriptures, or the sages of Antiquity, have set down in the books preserved for us by tradition."[20] The father's author-ity is behind Scripture and sermon as the stylus of writing, the rod of law, and even if a feminine Christ was the standard of "sentimental" preaching, as Emmons held, nevertheless the minister who preached in imitation of Christ aimed, Emmons said, as Christ did, to "lay open the blackness, turpitude, and malignity of the human heart."[21]

So Mrs. Stowe argued against the tradition of fathers when she

19. Nathaniel Emmons, *The Works of Nathaniel Emmons* (6 vols.; Boston, 1842), VI, Sermon 21, p. 281.
20. Foucault, *The Order of Things*, 33.
21. Emmons, *Works*, I, Sermon 1, p. 7.

wrote that "it is not a man's natural constitution, but the *use* he makes of it, which stamps him as good or vile" (*MW* 479). To her "the God of nature appears silent, unalterable, unsympathetic. . . . the silent inflexibility of God in upholding laws that work out such terrible agonies and suffering is something against which the human heart moans and chafes through all ancient literature" (*RS* 101). The text of sentimental fiction—Mrs. Stowe clarifies this as no other sentimental novelist did—set out to dissolve the paternal authority of theological language and to reinstall the maternal qualities of prayer and prophecy at the center of discourse, rather than the mathematical logic of the sermon.[22] She aimed to develop a language "not wrought-out by sharp-sided intellectual propositions, but melted in by divine fusion" (*MW* 396), a metaphoric discourse which anneals all difference, which supplements law with mediation.[23] There are, she says, "many languages of men,—but the language of prayer is one by itself, *in* all and *above* all. It is the inspiration of that Spirit that is ever working with our spirit, and constantly lifts us higher than we know," and in prayer which comes "when flesh and heart fail . . . he who prays is a prophet, and a mightier than he speaks in him. . . . 'the Spirit itself maketh intercession for us'" (*MW* 318).[24]

This privileged language is rooted in maternity, and it opposes the authority of fathers; so that "one verse in the Bible read by a mother in some hour of tender prayer has a significance deeper and higher than the most elaborate of sermons, the most acute of arguments" (*MW* 396). This requires a precisely maternal intervention—a computation which includes the Virgin's relationship with a feminized Christ; so that the authority of words could be shifted

22. For an excellent discussion of the ameliorization of American sermons, see Lawrence Buell, "The Unitarian Movement and the Art of Preaching in Nineteenth Century America," *American Quarterly*, XXIV (1972), 166–90; also David S. Reynolds, "From Doctrine to Narrative: The Rise of Pulpit Story-Telling in America," *American Quarterly*, XXXII (1980), 479–88.

23. See an important essay by Larzer Ziff, "The Literary Consequences of Puritanism," *English Literary History*, XXX (1963), 293–305.

24. On the uses of prayer and prophecy see James P. Walsh, "Holy Time and Sacred Space in Puritan New England, *American Quarterly*, XXXII (1980), 79–95.

from the father's inscription to the maternal voice which intercedes, mediates, and gives birth to a new utterance. Then the reign of a truly sentimental language will commence, "speaking almost unconsciously out of some higher sphere, and in higher language than that of earth" (RS 43).

In such a language as this "all the dearest forms of human affection are used to shadow forth what [Christ] will be to his people. He is to be the royal bridegroom, his willing people the bride" (RS 15). Accordingly, in the poetry of the Psalms, "the joy of every marriage suggested the joy of that divine marriage with a heavenly bridegroom" (RS 16). And under the promise of the New Testament "this Mediator, both divine and human," will "interpret the silence of God to man, who should be his WORD to his creatures" (RS 47). Christ turns back on Old Testament Scripture in a way that changes language itself: "He continually refers to them as writings that reflect his own image" (RS 68) (born of woman, carried under the mother's heart and voice): "When we read the Old Testament Scriptures we go along a track that we know Jesus and his mother must often have trod together," and she was "a prophetess, one whose mind was capable of the highest ecstasy of inspiration" (RS 98).[25]

Through the mother's presence the paternal authority of language becomes more than the inscription of law. The maternal heart becomes "spiritually clairvoyant. The way to God becomes clear and open" (RS 98). Then language too becomes *enceinte*— cinctured and cincturing rather than inscribed, an enclosure for the metaphor that will enchant, occupy, and quicken, which possesses its essence and its use and is brought forth to transfigure perception and feeling: "as the seed buried in the earth is to the new

---

25. For a concise and useful summary of Mrs. Stowe's heterodox faith, see Edward Wagenknecht, *Harriet Beecher Stowe: The Known and the Unknown* (New York, 1965), Chap. 11. See also Milton Rugoff, *The Beechers: An American Family in the Nineteenth Century* (New York, 1981), 291, 293, 359, for the heterodoxy of her siblings. The fullest study and the best remains Foster's *The Rungless Ladder*, esp. 108–28. The best recent study of theological subtlety in *The Minister's Wooing* is Lawrence Buell's "Calvinism Romanticized: Harriet Beecher Stowe, Samuel Hopkins, and *The Minister's Wooing*," *ESQ*, XXIV (1978), 119–32.

plant or flower, so is our present mortal body to the new immortal one that shall spring from it" (*RS* 107).

No doubt Mrs. Stowe was often enough the worst of authors—wooden, maudlin—but she wrote three excellent novels: *Uncle Tom's Cabin, The Minister's Wooing,* and *Oldtown Folks.* And parts of these are all but unbearable to modern tastes. They have in common with one another and with their countless ilk a set of predictable gestures and a burdensome vocabulary of feeling. But there is more to Mrs. Stowe's fiction. To be sure her literary colleagues manage little beyond the hyperbolic repetition of these stipulated forms. Their relationship to the theological code behind their own sentiment tends to be routine and unchanging. They are what they inherit. But in Mrs. Stowe at her best—and it is this rather than her sensibility that makes her important—the theological origin of literary conventions is made subtle and enchanting. She understood theology both as illusion and illumination. Theology is her true subject always, whereas with T. S. Arthur (say) one must understand literary conventions themselves to be the subject of a textual narcissism. Stowe reveals in a much more skillful way, with a genuine fascination, the assumptions she shares—but more consciously—with the other writers of sentimental fiction.

Her language and theirs constitutes a system of analogies between nature and the supernatural. As with Emerson, language is thus metaphoric in its essence; and at its best her understanding of metaphor and symbol is rich, even lavish. And we have no writer of fiction—not, I would argue, even Hawthorne—with a more brilliant and flexible understanding of American ecclesiastical history. She remains a minor figure because of her uneven accomplishments. But when she strikes the real antinomian key, and in rendering the dense and conflicted theological context within which her justification of desire develops, we recognize her as a native genius. Her figure for desire is the heart, and she drew her understanding of the heart's importance directly (as few other American writers did) from the theology of Jonathan Edwards and his followers. Moreover she developed what she found there on her own terms and out of her own long struggle with faith.

Edwards had said (and the dogma had long echoed in American thought) that what is "meant by them who affirm that virtue is founded in sentiment, and not in reason, [is] that they who see the beauty of true virtue do not perceive it by argumentation or its connections and consequences, but by the frame of their own minds, or a certain spiritual sense given them by God."[26] It is given by God, if it is given—but only those already resigned to the systematic reasoning of Edwardsean theology could be sure of such a sentimental reading. It depends on the logical displacement of natural, therefore fallen and depraved, sensibility. It is not spontaneous, and never unaided. The natural heart is deceiving. It requires to be prepared by "prolonged introspective meditation and self-analysis in the light of God's revealed Word," so that "from conviction of conscience, the soul moved through a series of interior stages . . . which in turn were intended to arouse a longing desire for grace."[27]

But no affection of the heart which does not first submit to a system of logic could be thus sanctified. Only those whose "disinterested benevolence" allowed them to accept the damnation of others—friends, loved ones, even themselves—in acknowledgment of man's depravity and in submission to "the good of being in general" might possess such a virtuous sentimental sense. What Edwards called "private affections . . . detached from general benevolence" could not serve: "No affection whatsoever, to any creature, or any system of created beings, which is not dependent on, nor subordinate to a propensity or union of the heart to God . . . can be of the nature of true virtue."[28]

Therefore Lyman Beecher advised his daughter Catherine, who had agonized for months over the sudden death of her fiancé—a death unmitigated by any evidence of regeneration—that her "feelings of insubmission" must be subordinated to "the resignation of necessity."[29] "The Bible has told you," he wrote her, "that your heart is deceitful, is desperately wicked . . . but now you hold it

26. Jonathan Edwards, *The Nature of True Virtue* (Ann Arbor, 1960), 99.
27. Norman Pettit, *The Heart Prepared: Grace and Conversion in Puritan Spiritual Life* (New Haven, 1966), 17.
28. Edwards, *The Nature of True Virtue*, 19, 23.
29. Barbara M. Cross (ed.), *The Autobiography of Lyman Beecher* (2 vols.; Cam-

bound to be conformed to the law, or even to the Gospel . . . you find it . . . impatient of restraint, violent, wayward, and ungovernable" (LB 365).[30] Remorselessly and lovingly he invited her to "consult your own cold, selfish heart" (LB 363) and to remember submission to the logic of system as the only sure response, whether to grace or to damnation: "God's way to produce obedience in sinners is to require it, and make them feel their obligation to render it, until excuses and evasions are cut off, until every mouth is stopped" (LB 363). The sinner having brought his unregenerate heart to this acceptance of God's authority—even if that authority demands the beloved's spiritual destruction—may then find a sanctified movement of the heart prepared by "obligation . . . [and] immediate duty"; but "to give other directions than those of immediate spiritual obedience is to take away from the sinner, and out of the hands of the Spirit, the means of grace" (LB 363).

A metaphorical arc over the concatenated logical chain; other directions—this freedom is what Mrs. Stowe uses the sentimental text to seek. She aims to make desire a possible means of grace; and in The Minister's Wooing, which develops her heterodox theology, we find, beneath the conventions and merely ornamental aspects of the tradition of sentiment, and precisely under the heart of an orthodox tradition, an absolutely metaphorical countertext which does just that—resanctifies the natural heart's desire. Her text shows how desire may be transformed into maternity as the heart is prepared for grace, and how this movement may transform the larger text of culture.

The Minister's Wooing dramatizes this radical claim, and we must bear in mind that the novel allegorizes a theological history and dilemma in order to resolve and reform them. The novel poses "a dramatic situation," Lawrence Buell argues, "in which a religion of doctrinal rigor, defined as the communal standard, is played off

---

bridge, Mass., 1961), 361. Subsequent references, abbreviated LB, will be given parenthetically in the text.

30. Rugoff, The Beechers, offers a lengthy account of Catherine's bereavement and religious struggle (45–53). See also Wagenknecht, Harriet Beecher Stowe, 36–37; Foster, The Rungless Ladder, 89–90; and Edmund Wilson, Patriotic Gore (New York, 1962), 38–42, for Stowe's use of this episode in The Minister's Wooing.

against a religion of love in such a way that the claims of both are deeply felt and the first is compromised but not discredited by the other."[31] Out of this context emerges a fiction concerned with the justification of desire, determined to provide the alibi which could exonerate desire. But of what? Of being merely "natural," of being the sign of man's distance from the divine will. But Mrs. Stowe means to celebrate desire as the sign rather of a possibility for those natural ecstatic feelings unclaimed or repudiated by the cold logic of Edwardsean theology. That was the problem of *The Minister's Wooing,* which chiefly narrates the story of Mary Scudder, a poor but accomplished and beautiful young woman who is courted by Dr. Samuel Hopkins (the influential follower of Jonathan Edwards); by James Marvyn, a dashing sailor whose romantic attractions are clear but whose spiritual condition is in doubt; and, briefly and improbably, by Aaron Burr, Jonathan Edwards' unregenerate grandson.

It is not enough to describe these characters solely as sentimental conventions—the virtuous older man who loves deeply but without erotic feeling; the maiden who is beautiful, saintly, and suffering; the darkly handsome youth whose clouded suit provides some interesting anxiety; the Byronic figure, whose sensibility is ruined by loose cynicism. As the stereotypes of a comic tradition looking back to Plautus and beyond they provide a familiar code of taboos and sanctions. But they become something more complex through their allegorical likeness—one might almost say their metaphorical identity—to a clearly understood set of theological counterparts. Every detail of *The Minister's Wooing,* whether of plot, theme, or style, bears on the plan and work of divine presence. It is "impossible," Mrs. Stowe says toward the middle of the novel, "to write a story of New England life and manners for superficial thought or shallow feeling. They who would fully understand . . . must go down with us to the very depths." In these depths one finds the theological context of metaphor: "Never was there a community where the roots of common life shot down so deeply, and were so intensely grappled around things sublime and eternal." At this

31. Buell, "Calvinism Romanticized," 129.

radical source, the constituting intelligence as well as the syntax of her culture, is the founding group of seekers, the fathers who "turned their backs on the whole glory of the visible," who went "straight to the heart of things" to confront "the problem of universal being."[32] The New England Puritans of whom she writes here do not "compare their maps of the Infinite" merely as "theory or speculation":

> New England was one vast sea, surging from depths to heights with thought and discussion on the most insoluble of mysteries . . . a foundation on which actual life was based with intensest earnestness. (MW 334)

This "seminal period" of New England history (as she termed it in her Preface to Oldtown Folks), the foundation and communal source which literary text shares with cultural text, was "consecrated." She saw it as a commonwealth where men "whose whole souls were in a state of fusion, by their conceptions of an endless life" (OF 51), safely "hedged in and defended the morality" of the community: "If there be such a thing possible as perfect faith in the eternal and invisible, and perfect loyalty to God and conscience, these men were pervaded by it" (OF 52).

This is the scene of her texts: theo/logical—word, speech, discourse of God; God-speaking. What Emerson and Whitman did for essays and poetry, Mrs. Stowe did for fiction: into a devotional tradition she inserted an ecstatic text which signified the recuperation of something lost since the Fall. This was, in a sense, what these intensely different writers shared—a discourse of the heart, of valorized feeling, prophecy, ecstasy, which accepted the potentially regenerative power of natural affections.

In this devotional context Dr. Hopkins represents nearly the most orthodox theology imaginable. "In those days," Mrs. Stowe reminds us, "the minister united in himself all those ideas of superior position and cultivation with which the theocratic system of the New England community had invested him." Hopkins was regarded "with something of the veneration which might have been

---

32. Harriet Beecher Stowe, Oldtown Folks, ed. Henry F. May (Cambridge, Mass., 1966), 47. Subsequent references will be identified by the abbreviation OF and given parenthetically in the text.

accorded a divine messenger" (*MW* 96), and even, occasionally, with rather more: "It is said that a little child once described his appearance in the pulpit by saying, 'I saw God there, and I was afraid'" (244).

No doubt. Hopkins' "early training had been all logical, not in the least aesthetic"; his style therefore "gave only the results of thought, not its incipient processes; and the consequence was, that few could follow him. . . . his religious teachings were characterized by an ideality so high as quite to discourage ordinary virtue" (*MW* 87). His extraordinary personal gentleness, compassion, and benevolence were always and famously evident, but they did not prevent him from preaching the "views of human existence" (334) which are centered by this dogma:

> The human race, without exception, coming into existence "under God's wrath and curse," with a nature so fatally disordered, that, although perfect free agents, men were infallibly certain to do nothing to Divine acceptance until regenerated by the supernatural aid of God's spirit,—this aid being given only to a certain decreed number of the human race, the rest, with enough free agency to make them responsible, but without this indispensable assistance exposed to the malignant assaults of evil spirits versed in every art of temptation, were sure to fall hopelessly into perdition. (335)

It is a strange sentence, surely, to find in a sentimental novel. The syntax and content are equally uncompromising and difficult, and perfectly set the problematic before us. Construction overdetermines the form, pauses, subordinates, underscores the sense of fragmentation and hopelessness which the theology insists on, fractures the sense, breaks it up, and only just reassembles it as a system. And the last clause moves directly down into a sonorous and dreadful end.

This entire chapter (23, "Views of Divine Government") is remarkable, brilliant, tracing the theological history of New England and putting it at the center of an otherwise routine literary mode where it illuminates and deepens the American sentimental universe. It gives terrible meaning to the otherwise undifferentiated suffering which so tediously opposes the power of desire in sentimental fiction, since Hopkins is, after all, at the center of courtship in the novel. We begin to see this as Mrs. Stowe goes on: "Dr.

Hopkins in many places distinctly recognizes . . . the greater part of the human race . . . had been eternally lost"; and "this amount of sin and suffering, being the best and most necessary means of the greatest final amount of happiness, was not merely permitted, but distinctly chosen, decreed, and provided for, as essential in the schemes of Infinite Benevolence" (MW 336). Therefore "it was always proposed to every inquiring soul, as an evidence of regeneration, that it should truly and heartily accept all the ways of God thus declared right and lovely, and from the heart submit to him as the only just and good"; and thus, she continues, "it will be seen what materials of tremendous internal conflict and agitation were all the while working in every bosom" (338).

In a subtle and complex passage (which Charles H. Foster has used to focus his excellent study of Mrs. Stowe), she puts the dilemma of Edwardsean theology very clearly:

> There is a ladder to heaven, whose base God has placed in human affections, tender instincts, symbolic feelings, sacraments of love, through which the soul rises higher and higher, refining as she goes, till she outgrows the human, and changes, as she rises, into the image of the divine. (MW 87)

This parturition of the soul, its transformation from the organ of instinct and feeling into something more evolved, "the image of the divine," is the most important aspect of structure shared by sentimental novels. The regeneration of fundamental human experience according to this strict theological model held that "the state of the heart determines whether the soul shall live in the light of divine truth."[33] It is right to say that such popular fiction "was designed . . . to provide channels for the unimpeded discharge of strong but crude feelings," but this discharge of feeling was also the sign of a regenerate heart and an escape from the relentless logic and reason of Calvinism; it is literature's case for the sanctification of desire.[34]

33. Pettit, The Heart Prepared, viii.
34. Henry Nash Smith, "The Scribbling Women and the Cosmic Success Story," Critical Inquiry, I (1974), 50. To be sure, Pettit shows that the reformed idea of the heart "was not a mystical conception. It did not derive from the Neoplatonic idea that man, through an effort of the will, may move from one level of spiritual activity to another until at last he becomes one with God. . . . This side of Augustinian piety . . . had been

This deeply heterodox privilege of emotion represents a radical alteration of Edwardsean theology, which even during the Great Revival submitted feeling to the most rigorous logical examination. It is true that we find sentimental fiction, like the theology of Charles Grandison Finney, "exalting feeling and imagination above reasoning and intellect," but in Mrs. Stowe this is a conscious strategy to represent a complex New England doubleness.[35] Here she deliberately juxtaposes the powers of system and sentiment in order to expose the limitation of Edwardsean logic. How complex and damaging she felt the repression of feeling to be comes gradually clear in this extended passage: "At the very top of this ladder," she goes on, is "that celestial grade where the soul knows self no more, having learned . . . how blest it is to lose herself in that eternal Love and Beauty." It is this final translation of desire, desire as loss of the self in a fusion with "eternal Love and Beauty," that is the end of God's design as she and sentimentalism see it: an identification with spiritual oneness, "to raise the soul to which the Eternal Father organized every relation of human existence and strung every cord of human love . . . to which all its multiplied powers tend." And she concludes, "this Ultima Thule of virtue had been seized upon by Dr. Hopkins as the *all* of religion. He knocked out every round of the ladder but the highest, and then, pointing to its hopeless splendors, said to the world, 'Go up thither and be saved!'" (*MW* 87–88).

This, according to Mrs. Stowe's interpretation, is the dilemma of Edwardsean theology and the text of American culture: it puts grace out of the reach of love and the intentional soul, and thus cancels desire, the longing for what is lost, just at the point where it might develop from instinct into regeneration. This is the exclusion of desire by a system which is nonetheless based on it, and Hop-

virtually discarded by the Reformers." (*The Heart Prepared*, 15). But Mrs. Stowe understands this displacement of Augustine by Calvinist paternalism: "The clear logic and intense individualism of New England deepened the problems of the Augustinian faith, while they swept away all those softening provisions so earnestly clasped to the throbbing heart of that great poet of theology" (*MW* 341).

35. Perry Miller, *The Life of the Mind in America: From the Revolution to the Civil War* (New York, 1965), 32.

kins, whose disappointment at losing his own heart's desire raises "an ocean-tempest . . . [a] boiling sea of passion" (*MW* 552), comes himself to incorporate the theological paradox which Mrs. Stowe's fiction sets out to correct. He proposes to Mary and is accepted submissively by her. But her heart's love, believed lost at sea, returns. Submissive to the law of fathers, she does not seek release from her vow to marry Hopkins. Yet her preference for the younger hero is clear, the difference between desire and law is unmistakable, and Hopkins is made to recognize it. The demand of the fiction faces the demand of theology: her readers, Mrs. Stowe imagines, will be "particularly set against the success of our excellent orthodox hero, and bent on reminding us of the claims of that unregenerate James" (181). By preferring James the novel corrects theology, then, and not without a certain measure of violence. Hopkins' will "that he thought wholly subdued seemed to rise under him as a rebellious giant. A few hours before, he thought himself established in an invincible submission to God's will that nothing could shake. Now he looked into himself as into a seething vortex of rebellion" (552).

Whether or not we credit the language with a measure of phallic suggestiveness, Hopkins' response to the strength of his own desire is instructive. In spite of the violence of his disappointment he determines to subordinate desire to logic, and to resubmit his will to God's; "and, taking his Concordance, began busily tracing out and numbering all the proof-texts for one of the chapters of his theological system! till, at last, he worked himself down to such calmness that he could pray" (*MW* 552–53).

So much the better for Hopkins, whose logic and discipline grant him an alternative to the desire that promises to save sinners more democratically than his dogma. His theology suits his reason; his reason schools his passion. But we are, nevertheless, repeatedly invited to ask exactly how his "perfect logic of life" (*MW* 184) differs from that of Aaron Burr, whose unscrupulous seduction of the young Madame de Frontignac is a counterpoint to Hopkins' courtship of Mary. Burr begins in French, "that language whose very structure in its delicate *tutoiement* gives such . . . shade after shade of intimacy and tenderness," until his victim answers recklessly with words "which carried with them all the warmth of that sacred fire which is given to woman to light and warm the temple of home, and which sears and scars when kindled from any other shrine" (228). Prevented from advancing the seduction by Mary, who turns his compliments and briefly moves "the diviner part of him" to tears, Burr nonetheless feels his coldly rational habits "slowly stealing back round his heart" (479). In fact Burr "has no religion in his heart" (395), and this tragically excludes him from even so generous a grace as Mrs. Stowe would wish to allow: to suppress his convulsive crisis of feeling "he set himself vigorously to some columns of arithmetical calculations" (419).

The difference between Hopkins and Burr is manifest; finally, "the one watched against his better nature as the other did against his worse"; but there is a similarity between them that signifies almost as much. "Both had a perfect *logic* of life, and guided themselves with an inflexible rigidity by it" (*MW* 482). In this each comes perilously close to the novel's most reprehensible character, the obstinate slaver Simeon Brown, for whom "logic was everything. . . . to perceive a truth and not act in logical sequence from it [was] a thing so incredible, that he had not yet engendered his capacity to take it as a possibility" (152–53). Brown perceives only the truth apparent to the reason. He is a grotesque version of the dangerous faculty which Hopkins and Burr privilege in different degrees. Neither of them can admit desire—the spiritual quickening of the heart toward what has been lost—as a means for the self's salvation. Burr for instance recalls his mother (much as Simon Legree does in Chapter 35 of *Uncle Tom's Cabin*) as if she "held up before him a glass in which he saw himself white-robed and crowned, and so dazzling in purity that he loathed his present self," but he resists the icon, and turns toward his imperial version of desire by sitting down to consider "some maps of new territories . . . till his mind was as dry and his pulse as calm as a machine" (419). Typically, his rational talent represses the maternal influence; "His very mother might shrink in her grave to have him laid beside her" (302).[36]

36. On Mrs. Stowe's use of Aaron Burr, see Wilson, *Patriotic Gore*, 49.

Burr "drilled down and subjugated a nature of singular richness" (*MW* 482), and Dr. Hopkins, Mrs. Stowe reminds us more than once, "had practised his subtle mental analysis till his instruments were so fine-pointed and keen-edged that he scarce ever allowed a flower of sacred emotion to spring in his soul without picking it to pieces to see if its genera and species were correct" (289). This is his rectification of nature, and of desire: the rational instrument of dissection, logical, fine-pointed, keen-edged—cutting to the heart—is also the stylus of writing, "animated by an unflinching consistency which never shrank from carrying an idea to its remotest logical verge" (336), she says of Hopkins, that "with calculating shrewdness *uses* [the] most touching miracle of love only to corrupt and destroy the loving" (302), she says of Burr—inscribing texts "so terrific in their refined poetry of torture" (this of Jonathan Edwards) "that few persons of quick sensibility could read them through without agony" (337).

Out Hopkins, out Burr, disciple and grandson of Edwards. Both fall beyond the full privilege of desire in sentimental fiction, though both are irresistible types of the genre. Hopkins is saved and Burr is damned by the same reason, carried to the "remotest logical verge." Neither provides a full enough scope for the experiment of Mrs. Stowe's sentiment. They fascinate but cannot focus her text; they fail to provide an appropriate scene for desire. What has desire to do, finally, with their calculus, with logic, reason, sequence? These are not what is lost to desire, they are what replace that loss and hide it. God's love is desire's loss.[37]

And that leaves James Marvyn, "a formidable irruption" into the "steady, decorous, highly-respectable" context of orthodox New England, who even at birth "was an infant of moods and tenses, and those not of any regular verb" (*MW* 107), "held as little better than an infidel and a castaway by the strict religious circles in his native place" (26); and Mary, who lives "that vivid life in the soul and sentiment which resists the chills of analysis, as a healthful human heart resists cold" (289). James Russell Lowell recognized

37. See Buell, "Calvinism Romanticized," 122, 124.

James as a character "in whose heart the wild religion of nature swells till the strait swathings of Puritanism are burst" and Mary as one "in whom Cupid is to try conclusions with Calvin."[38] Lowell puts it clearly: James makes necessary and Mary makes possible the redemption of nature by desire, and the violence and eccentricity associated with James signify both the necessity and the means of discovering a new value of desire, and a new way of expressing it. What Leo Bersani says about the hero of desire applies here: such heroes not only search out (as Bersani says) but are "a violent passage from one psychological and social order to another." They seek through the violence they embody "the continuities and the coherent patterns of desire which condemn [them] to a life of repetitions"; so James, like Bersani's hero, reveals an "escape from tragedy"—from desire as suffering and ruination.[39] But for Mrs. Stowe such energy requires a focus. Without Mary, James's relationship to reality would consist only of a series of gestures, whether of frustration, apostasy, or despair—the familiar tropes of modern literature, from which Mary Scudder's modification of theological tradition manages to shield him and to which, like the culture at large, he has been driven by the tyranny of logic over the heart.

Certainly systematic theology can do nothing for James or the power he is meant to evoke. For him, as he says, "it's all a maze. . . . I think it rather makes me worse; and then they tell me it's because I'm a natural man, and the natural understandeth not the things of the Spirit. Well, I *am* a natural man,—how's a fellow to help it?" (*MW* 34). James is a "wild . . . uncanonical" person (185), as much and as thoroughly "a creature of this material world as Mary was of the invisible and heavenly" (132); but for one of the "priests . . . among women," one who could "recognize the divine original" (131)—one "inspired by a divine gift of prophecy,—like the mother of St. Augustine" (130)—it is possible to recognize "the divine ideal of our nature" (130) in James. This is a desire of the soul,

38. Cited in Charles Edward Stowe, *The Life of Harriet Beecher Stowe* (Boston, 1889), 330.

39. See Leo Bersani, *A Future for Astyanax: Character and Desire in Literature* (Boston, 1976), 4, 50.

a kind of clairvoyance which sees through the "treacherous . . . dreadful, inexplicable" mysteries "of all the harpings of Nature" (68) and rarely "bears any sort of relation to the reality of the object" (128).

For as James says when he writes Mary—setting himself opposite to Dr. Hopkins and refiguring nature and natural feeling— "there has been another history going on within me" (*MW* 515). A new alternative is revealed to him by the passage in Genesis concerning Jacob (the name is a variant of James) and his vision of a ladder—an image which quite supplants Hopkins' rungless ladder with another one: "And he dreamed, and behold the angels of God ascending and descending on it" (Genesis 28:12). The vision clarifies presence for James as well as for Jacob; as James says, "That was a sight which came to the very point of his necessities. He saw that there was a way between him and God. . . . *there* was something that looked to me like a tangible foundation to begin upon" (517). The dream opens a transcendent path; it puts a sign before the unregenerate consciousness of nature and commences the process by which spiritual meaning suffuses natural perception. It makes the space of James's subjectivity a sacred one, and thus, as Mircea Eliade suggests in his reading of Jacob's dream, "implies a hierophany, an irruption of the sacred that results in detaching a territory from the surrounding cosmic milieu and making it qualitatively different." And it is motivated by desire—by James's sense of his distance from Mary, both literally and spiritually. So the "communication with heaven, the paradoxical point of passage from one mode of being to another" which Jacob's ladder (and James's) constitutes, ensues from the closure of an absence. The motive of desire discovers and is provoked by the Father's messenger and therefore becomes an occasion for struggling with His authority to subordinate by means of law: Mrs. Stowe interpreted the enigmatic figure which appeared to Jacob as an Old Testament manifestation of Christ (*RS* 4–6), the "pitying Friend and Saviour" (*RS* 6), the "mysterious Word, this divine Son, this Revealer of God in the Old Testament" (*RS* 2). It is a beginning for the figurative cure, since "In such cases the *sign*, fraught with religious meaning, introduces an absolute element and puts an end to relativity and confusion."[40] This offer of a sign, that paradoxical passageway between rival orders of reality, begins to transform the centrifugal energy of being into a brilliant implosion toward understanding, natural affection, and freedom from a depraved origin of desire.

James guesses, rightly, that Dr. Hopkins "would have called that all selfishness" (MW 517)—not "the gate of heaven" as it is to Jacob (28:17), who later comes to see God "face to face" (33:30), but the interpretation "of a creature in conscious rebellion to its Eternal Sovereign" (89). To James, however, the visionary image signifies "a new life" (519) and the conviction that Scripture is a transcendent as well as a regulating language. He writes Mary that he returns to New England "quite another man . . . with a whole new world of thought and feelings in my heart" (520).[41]

Like prayer and prophecy, his letter provides an aperture within systematic theology. It dissolves the specter of a soul both damned and unaided by law, virtuous in itself but helpless to reach what man is nonetheless obliged by the God of fathers to find, that "saintly elevation" which constitutes an absolute difference, so that "all earthly fairness and grandeur are but the dim type, the distant shadow" (MW 88) of divine fullness. Mary has, we already know, "small care for [the] logical relations" of systematic theology. The "glacial reasonings" (342) of its punitive equations horrify her sensibility. The report of James's sudden death forces her to realize that according to Hopkins' dogma "No rite, no form, no paternal relation . . . interposed the slightest shield between the trembling spirit and Eternal Justice. The individual entered eternity alone, as if he had no interceding relation in the universe" (341). In despair she feels "as if the point of a wedge were being driven . . . between her and her God" (344–45).

But James's wonderful reappearance, his vision and understanding, and the epistolary text of his heterodox conversion restore the fullness of her sentimental power and begin what is apparently nec-

40. Mircea Eliade, *The Sacred and the Profane: The Nature of Religion,* trans. Willard R. Trask (New York, 1961), 26, 27.

41. See Murray G. Murphey, "The Psychodynamics of Puritan Conversion," *American Quarterly,* XXXI (1979), 135–47, for a convincing discussion of conversions which genuinely alter personalities.

essary to the rehabilitation of her desire, the development of the maternal icon. Upon first seeing James, Mary is literally ecstatic: "whether in the body or out of the body God knoweth, she felt herself borne in those arms, and words . . . profaned by being repeated, were in her ear" (*MW* 506). While she feels herself "borne" James holds her "as tenderly as a mother holds her babe" and "they spoke of love mightier than death . . . of yearnings,—of longing prayers . . . and then of this great joy," the "love which death cannot quench" (507).

This ecstatic language begins by assembling the signifiers of erotic desire and submitting them to a test. Arms, words, an embrace, passion and a temptation lead to the momentary displacement of the soul by the flesh. The reunion of James and Mary takes place outside their memory of the law. But the death mentioned twice is the law's shadow, a threat that still faces desire—so the love they spontaneously declare is immediately qualified and bounded, and the body's ecstasy is only a problem. The representation of feeling is therefore instantly spiritualized: its conventional symbols defend it against fulfillment; they find a sacrificial meaning for desire, rather than its gratification: it is the quenchless love beyond death.

But their love has another dimension as well—the strangely irresistible maternity which even James's embrace suggests. He is as tender as a mother. The metaphor both expresses and controls his desire, and grants it a special privilege and promise; though outside any rational meaning (this is just the point), it promises a higher arbitration than that of logic. In James the mother is manifest; and in the mother Christ, the son who realizes the father's love. The metaphor bonds the complex theological power which begins to take shape toward the end of the novel. It is like a palimpsest which reveals a transcendent experience reaching through reason to love, beyond the body to a bodiless ideal. Then ecstasy returns safely, fully metaphorized, with the spiritualized love that Mary comes to feel after James has left her alone to read the account of his regeneration. She "rose, after reading this letter, in a divine state of exaltation,—the pure joy, in contemplating an infinite good to another, in which the question of self was utterly forgotten" (*MW* 521). This is the experience which echoes and supplants the ecstasy of the body; this is the soul's own ecstatic translation beyond the limits of desire, free of the threat of any death.

So that first vulnerable ecstasy which "choked," "throbbed," which seemed "a trance of blissful rest" (*MW* 506), is overcome by the shadow of the covenant. The bliss which both of them feel—"neither of them knew or felt anything but the great joy of being there side by side" (507)—is a charm broken by Mary's recollection that she has given herself "before God" (526) into the paternal custody of Dr. Hopkins, who possesses "her devoted filial love" (538). What remains for her legitimately to feel is something quite distinct from the body's joy. If she cannot be a desiring wife, she can be a saint. Of her brief hours in James's arms, "she thought God must have given them . . . to remind her of His love, and to strengthen her in the way of duty" (510), to keep her from "covenant-breaking . . . one of the vilest sins of humanity" (536). There is some comfort for Mary, but it is cold, in knowing that James will be "what she had always hoped and prayed he would be . . . that true and virtuous man, that Christian able to subdue life . . . a perfect and healthy manly nature, a reflection of the image of the superhuman excellence" (521). It is not so simple; it is nothing trivial, this redemption of nature through a desire that requires to be both romantic and spiritual, to be, in T. S. Arthur's phrase, "twofold . . . inextricably blended."

But James is able to remind Mary of the theology of sentiment, moving into the place of law: "Is it doing right to [Dr. Hopkins] to let him marry you in ignorance of the state of your feelings? . . . when the best and noblest part of your affections is gone wholly beyond your control?" (*MW* 533). His reasoning turns the process of Puritan examination neatly around; ecstasy has some purpose after all. Mary has known all along that as his wife she would be "the adoring companion of Infinite Beauty and Infinite Love" (313). Meanwhile, "I took knowledge of you, that you have been with Jesus," he tells her (519). Her intercession saves him, and his saves her: she escapes death in the law, and he accepts her as "the gentle guiding force that led [him] from . . . the habits of this world to the higher conception of an heroic and Christ-like manhood . . . brooding peacefully with dovelike wings over his soul, and he grew up under it noble in purpose and strong in spirit" (568).

And Mary feels, it might be said, that James is "the loveliest character that ever unfolded through childhood and youth to manhood" (RS 31), that she knows him "perfectly, entirely, intimately . . . [that] his life grew out of her immortal nature" (RS 36), and that she may thus "possess the beloved object in perfect security, guarded by a divine promise" (RS 32). It is as if, in exchange for what she teaches him, he "gave birth to new conceptions of love; to a fervor, a tenderness, of which before the human soul scarce knew its own capacity" (RS 33).

This language would perfectly clarify the courtship of James and Mary; it accurately describes what each is to the other; but in fact it appears not in *The Minister's Wooing* but in *Religious Sketches*, in Mrs. Stowe's analysis of Christ's relation to His mother. It is not easy to distinguish Mary from Mary, wife from mother. Indeed it is not always possible. Their functions identify with one another. Mary Scudder's "essentially Hebrew education" (MW 473) provides the "calm, immutable center on which she rested" (264); she resembles paintings "of the girlhood of the Virgin" (19), a "youthful Mother of Sorrow" in a European cathedral (36). In his moments of temptation, James tells her, "your image has stood between me and . . . vice," because "you represent to me a sphere higher and holier than any in which I have ever moved" (70). For James the "invisible world of religion is unreal" (32), but this unreality can be mediated by "one of the great company . . . who are priests unto God,—ministering between the Divine One, who has unveiled himself unto them, and those who as yet stand in outer courts of the great sanctuary of truth and holiness" (74). Even Aaron Burr reminds Mary, "You must intercede for us" (220), and James makes her value even more clear: "If, through your prayers, your Bible, your friendship, you can bring me to your state, I am willing to be brought here,—nay, desirous. God has put the key of my soul into your hands" (73). Mary responds in turn with what Mrs. Stowe describes as "the most solemn and touching thought" possible: "to feel the immortality of a beloved soul hanging upon us, to feel that its only communication with Heaven must be through us" (73).

Mary's function is to attract desire, to claim the desire of the unregenerate Other and to redeem, by her intercession between nature and God, what would, by orthodox standards, always fall outside of grace; to constitute and provide a sign of desire through which gratification escapes itself, gives up bliss for adoration, holiness, immortality. Through her incarnation of metaphor desire acquires a structure, freedom from its natural cycle. This sign of maternity is "a threshold where 'nature' confronts 'culture,'" where nature as desire becomes culture as maternity—where instinct chooses to submit itself to law, where law becomes irreducible, where the wife is refigured as chaste, inviolate, so that within the icon of the mother one order of reality, intensely represented as a passionate erotic relationship, is exchanged for another order of greater value, expressed through that figure of chastity and mediation which is deliberately placed and held beyond ambivalence or ambiguity, beyond desire itself. It is "the movement of a birth, the continuous advent of *presence* . . . [a] moment of pure continuity . . . between the time of desire and the time of pleasure."[42] Through the icon of the mother, significance transmits itself without friction in either direction: word is made flesh, flesh is made spirit; difference is dissolved. Desire becomes transparent, then evanescent, and the marriage festival is made continuous, the rite of metaphor, a celebration in which two are made one and that unity is endlessly sustained as an ideal. Language produces an image which offers reciprocity without the threat of violation:

> The fair poetic maiden, the seeress, the saint, has passed into that appointed shrine for woman, more holy than cloister, more saintly and pure than church or altar,—*a Christian home.* Priestess, wife, and mother, there she ministers daily in holy works of household peace, and by faith and prayer and love redeems from grossness and earthliness the common toils and wants of life. (*MW* 567–68)

But there is another view. Maternal representation can also reveal (Julia Kristeva says of Bellini's paintings of Madonna and Son) "a *remnant,* which cannot be found in the . . . serenely positioned, maternal body . . . intermediary and passageway." The remnant is

---

42. Jacques Derrida, *Of Grammatology,* trans. Gayatri Chakravorty Spivak (Baltimore, 1976), 262–63.

the energy of the infant Christ, who appears (in Bellini, she argues) to be strenuous beyond the son's limits, because he is charged to be husband as well as son. He is the son who has fathered himself, who has therefore already possessed what becomes forbidden to him. Consequently, he is always a metaphor of an excluded value, an unnamable value: a desire that must be set aside. The son's doubling of the father's desire, always latent in Christian theology, is "precisely what constitutes the enigma of Christian maternity. . . . such an unnamable . . . is not *less* but *more* than Word and Meaning. It is the recovered meaning of the incestuous son—the artist."[43] This is not Mrs. Stowe's maternity, but it is Melville's.

For Bellini, then, and for Melville, to represent the mother and her son is to supplement them with more than language allows, to constitute the mother as an image of desire that is not only maternal but (always?) also "intense, pre-Oedipal, predating the father." One's representation of the mother must look to possess her for oneself, then. But a representation of the father re-members him and subordinates the son. Perhaps it is true as a rule (it is in *Pierre*) that the representation of fathers annexes and appropriates the son's power, as if it were a burnt offering. This is a matter of succession, not transcendence: the son does not in fact become the father; he is the one who follows, serves, who resurrects the father's presence by sacrificing the self. The remnant Kristeva writes of is an image of the son who is always in his mother's arms; it is the son's attempt to make himself felt, known, admitted to an embrace by that inviolable serenity which is the mother's pose and mask. This remnant is a fragment of the father; it is the desire which always means to have come first, and which begins to realize incest rather than to repress it; it is a paradox meant to epitomize the rich inconsistency of Christianity, Kristeva comments, "by breathing into it, more than before, what it represses: the joyous serenity of incest with the mother."[44] This is another version of the relationship, outside of logic, outside of rule, which originates Christian theology and its literature, and speculates on the problem of nature and of

43. Julia Kristeva, "The Father, Love, and Banishment," in Roudiez (ed.), *Desire in Language,* 156.
44. *Ibid.,* 157, 156.

human instinct. It is implicit in the identification of Father and Son, in instinct repressed by sacrifice and rationalized by theology. It expresses the simultaneous difference and mutuality of soul and body, deferral and desire. Can this serene incest be recovered, spoken, sustained as the source of an original creative language? That investigation is the scandalous experiment of *Pierre*.

CHAPTER III

Incest and Language in *Pierre*

The crime consists in transgressing the semantic rule, in creating homonymy: the act *contra naturam* is exhausted in an utterance of counter-language, the family is no more than a lexical area, but this reduction is in no way immaterial: it guarantees the strongest of traditions, that of language, its full outrage: to transgress is to name outside the lexical division.

—Roland Barthes, *Sade, Fourier, Loyola*

What best opposes the transcendence of Mrs. Stowe's sentimental style is Melville's use of language in *Pierre* (1852). Here the informing myths of literature and indeed language itself seem to be breaking down, thanks to the involvement of Melville's hero in an incestuous relationship. This act of incest, whether real or imaginary, dissolves the taxonomies upon which the romantic sensibility most relied. Put more simply, the tradition romanticism uses to express and verify its universe is both examined and broken into fragments thanks to Pierre's violation of the incest taboo. Together with this fragmentation—a violation so important to Melville that it can only be represented as a myth of origin—goes a major reorientation of language. This reorientation becomes necessary because incest neutralizes the principle of reciprocal exchange upon which all structures, myth and language as well as kinship systems, are predicated. The fundamental basis of relationship is thus effaced, and Melville emphasizes this effacement, as Mrs. Stowe did her inscription, with his use of metaphor. From the opening of the novel, where the threat of incest is implied in apparently innocent uses of language, to the vision of Enceladus the Titan that marks the end of writing for Pierre, and so on to the apocalyptic conclusion, the text calls its own significance continually into question.

The theme of incest is immediately implied and ramified. Pierre, we are told, feels a "romantic filial love" for his mother (the paradox of incest could not be more succinctly stated) and has "more than once" sworn "a playful malice" toward any man who might indulge "insane hopes of wedding this unattainable being" for whom, since his father's death, "a reverential and devoted son seemed lover enough."[1] The edenic estate in which he dwells, the family home of Saddle Meadows, is thus a paradise in more than its pastoral setting: it is a symbolic locus where the son may enjoy the mother without rivalry or intervention. Yet—and this is important to keep in mind—this paradise is a derived estate, not an original one: its language, both pastoral and sentimental, is constituted primarily by literary cliches, and its authority is drawn from a father whose absence is only mitigated by the arts of portraiture and memory.[2] In this place language and kinship are determined by what is defunct. The pastoral place will later give way to a version of hell, though at the beginning Pierre is "surrounded by scenery whose uncommon loveliness was the mould of a delicate and poetic mind" (5).

But even this early in the novel the pun on "mould" begins to corrode the original meaning of the sentence. "Nothing," Melville writes a few pages later, "can be more significant of decay than the idea of corrosion" (9). Form, in fact order of any sort, inevitably gives way to the process of decay; derivation and corruption are inseparable. There are countless such puns in Melville's style, not only in *Pierre* but in each of his texts, and they generally suggest a darkness beneath the literal surface: they are the shadow that is always cast by writing.

1. Herman Melville, *Pierre; or, The Ambiguities,* ed. Harrison Hayford, Hershel Parker, and G. Thomas Tanselle (Evanston, 1971), 15. Subsequent references will be given parenthetically in the text.

2. On the pastoral opening, see Eric J. Sundquist, *Home as Found: Authority and Genealogy in Nineteenth-Century American Literature* (Baltimore, 1979), 150; and Henry Murray's Introduction to the Hendricks House edition of *Pierre* (New York, 1949), xxxvi.

What this pun reveals as it turns the meaning is that writing may, in certain circumstances, indicate a violent and dangerous opposition to the sanctity of language. Language may be doubled. And this divisive energy exists in the most transparent and familiar of languages as well as in the interdicted subject to which Melville will turn soon enough: *Et in arcadia ego* is the secret motto of the novel's beginning. The introduction of incest is preceded by an episode in which we are introduced to the sheerly conventional language of sentimental fiction and to a naïve emotion that is subsequently deepened as language and kinship turn toward the darkness of origins. Here Pierre encounters, in the silence of a nature entirely in repose, his fiancée Lucy Tartan, an "invoking angel" of the type common to the therapeutic literary mode of Mrs. Stowe, which transforms desire into redemption. But Lucy and the style she represents only mask a more compelling motive that has not yet been made clear, a desire which, once the opportunity presents itself, Pierre is ruinously quick to embrace. When in the coy language of sentiment Lucy asks Pierre why lovers swear oaths of affection, he replies "Because in us love is profane, since it mortally reaches toward the heaven in ye!" (4). Like the pun on mould, this opens to a problem that is at this point set in a barely discernible future. We will see, in Pierre's vision of Enceladus the Titan, what man's desire for the heavenly essence entails—particularly when it transforms the desire of sentimental fiction into incest. The corrosion suggested by Melville's pun will by this time have corrupted the "delicate and poetic mind" and the "uncommon loveliness" of the pastoral dream—and all other derived forms, including language and the novel—as well.

For the moment, however, the surface of his "green and golden world" (3) is all that Pierre can know. Yet even here there is a distance between his naïve perception of this world and what interpretation reveals. Just as it is possible to glimpse, behind the pun and the idealizing desire, a doubled and ironic second voice, it is possible to see—as William Braswell pointed out a quarter of a century ago—that Melville's style is a parody of the sentimental novel.[3] And of course the parody suggests that the universe in

3. William Braswell, "The Early Love Scenes of Melville's *Pierre*," *American Litera-*

which the novel appears to open is obsolete, that its language is already invalid, capable of being called into question. This being the case we should pay close attention to what the double inscriptions imply, especially about the desire which the fiction of domestic sentiment naïvely represents. And here we are led again to the theme of incest. Pierre and his mother, with a "strange license which a perfect confidence and mutual understanding at all points, had long bred between them . . . were wont to call each other brother and sister" (5). This curious confusion of kinship roles is underscored by a desire deflected away from the sentimental wife and expressed in a metaphor of language: "So perfect to Pierre had long seemed the illuminated scroll of his life thus far, that only one hiatus was discoverable by him in that sweetly-writ manuscript. A sister had been omitted from the text. . . . nor could the fictitious title, which he so often lavished upon his mother, at all supply the absent reality" (7).

What has already happened in the opening pages? We are first introduced to Lucy, the parody of an erotic stereotype; then to a widowed mother jealously guarded and possessed by her son; then to a mother who is also a sibling; and finally to Pierre's desire for a sister, "the second best gift of a man. . . . He who is sisterless, is as a bachelor before his time. For much that goes to make up the deliciousness of a wife, already lies in the sister" (7). "Lies," indeed; this too is a desire which means something other than it seems to, whose signification depends on the possibility of corrosive doubling. Melville's strategy is clear: both desire and words begin to suggest a dangerous second sense that amounts to another aspect of significance, another version of the self concealed within a language that is above all symptomatic rather than therapeutic. A legitimate erotic choice, ridiculed by parody, is displaced by forbidden options in much the same way as language permits the corrosive second sense to displace an original one. Melville's puns, arch though they may be, double in a consistent way. They darken legitimate kinships, which become confused with (and by) forbidden ones. In every case, moreover, the doubling occludes what is

---

ture, XXII (1950), 283–89. See also Sundquist, *Home as Found,* Chap. 4, *passim,* and esp. 158, 172, 175, 181–82.

given or derived. The conventional scene of narrative fiction; the mother released by the father's absence; the lover chosen under the mother's approval; the sister held in the bonds of kinship; the essence beyond the mortal object: these are cast into shadow by a language which blurs all stipulated relationships. Pierre's life is flawed by the "hiatus . . . the absent reality" of the one all-signifying relation which would culminate the others. The rest of the novel is an attempt to supplement or interpret these problematic relationships, to regain what has been lost by the violation of what has been given. But our investigation of that quest cannot proceed without some consideration of incest itself.

Kinship systems—rules of marriage—invariably begin, according to Lévi-Strauss, with a prohibition against incest. This prohibition marks man's first emergence out of nature into culture. With the incest taboo, he distinguishes an absolutely free condition from a way of living that is subject to laws. Whatever is both spontaneous and universal, Lévi-Strauss argues, must have its origin in nature; whatever is subject to rule is a sign of culture. The incest prohibition "constitutes a rule . . . which, alone among all the social rules, possesses at the same time a universal character."[4] The prohibition against incest is thus precisely on the frontier between nature and culture, and partakes of both; it is what ties man to his biological beginnings in nature and, at the same time, separates him from nature once and for all. "Perhaps the most drastic mutilation which man's erotic life has in all time experienced," as Freud says, this "first, totemic, phase" of civilization is a trace of man's lost origin in a free and richly open universe, but at the same time the inescapable law which prescribes all social behavior.[5] A violation of this principle would thus be the means by which man could return to nature—a condition whose freedom he dreams of as a total accommodation and plenitude, but which is, on the contrary (as

4. Claude Lévi-Strauss, *The Elementary Structures of Kinship*, trans. James Harle Bell, John Richard von Sturmer, and Rodney Needham, ed. Rodney Needham (Rev. ed.; Boston, 1969), 8–9. Unless otherwise indicated, all references to Lévi-Strauss are to this work and will be given parenthetically in the text.

5. James Strachey (ed.), *The Standard Edition of the Complete Psychological Works of Sigmund Freud*, trans. James Strachey *et al.* (24 vols.; London, 1953–74), XXI, 104.

Melville finally represents it), a "wide and wanton spoil" (344), what de Sade called "*une puissance sans raison ni sagesse.*"[6]

What exactly does the incest taboo accomplish for culture? For one thing, it allows humankind to find a way of increasing the dangerously restricted possibilities of marriage within a narrow range of blood-related partners to the immeasurably wider possibilities offered by marriage with strangers outside one's blood kin. Exogamy must initially have been a way of survival, Lévi-Strauss argues, since giving up the right to take closely related wives, and agreeing systematically to exchange them for women similarly denied to others, gains primitive man the right to claim a greater abundance of women with whom to increase his numbers, as well as a network of political *ententes.* Indeed, this reciprocal exchange may bring alliance into being. Such a system of exchange has as its most highly positive effect the prevention of social fragmentation: the "biological group" of blood relations "can no longer stand apart, and the bond of alliance with another family ensures the dominance of the social over the biological, and of the cultural over the natural" (479). As Lévi-Strauss says in *The Scope of Anthropology,* "The prohibition against incest creates bonds of alliance between these biological groups, the first such bonds which one can call social. The incest prohibition is thus the basis of human society: in a sense it is the society."[7]

The formation of biological groups into kinship systems, however, is merely a practical application of an infrastructural principle, one which determines other areas of exchange as well; and we must not overlook the fact that it is, first and foremost, the rule, the possibility of prohibition itself, that is significant. Kinship relations are only the evidence of this rule of reciprocity, which arises from a proscription against the absolute license of nature and of the individual to keep to himself. And this mandated exogamy is not simply a "rule of reciprocity" (51) but "the archetype of all other manifestations based upon reciprocity" (481). For Lévi-Strauss, ex-

6. Quoted in Josué Harari, "Exogamy and Incest: De Sade's Structures of Kinship," *Modern Language Notes,* LXXXVII (1973), 1216.

7. Claude Lévi-Strauss, *The Scope of Anthropology,* trans. Sherry Ortner Paul and Robert A. Paul (London, 1967), 2.

ogamous exchange is the original model upon which the mediation between any pairing of irreconcilable opposites is based, like the mediation, for example, between the opposing poles of language, metaphor and metonymy.[8] Thanks to this rule of mediation, which determines the function of all structures, the natural condition which "had been merely a huge distorted science became organized in grammatical terms involving a coercive charter for all conceivable ways of setting up and maintaining a reciprocity structure."[9]

In a wonderfully obscure passage, Lévi-Strauss explains and complicates the analogy between language and kinship in terms of the sign. Women, he says, "are not primarily a sign of social value, but a natural stimulant; and the stimulant of the only instinct the satisfaction of which can be deferred, and consequently the only one for which, in the act of exchange, and through the awareness of reciprocity, the transformation from the stimulant to the sign can take place, and, defining by this fundamental process the transformation from nature to culture, assume the character of an institution" (62–63). In other words—and other words are certainly called for—the deferral of desire for certain prohibited women opens an area where women become the first means of discourse. In the space of this deferral of desire, in this hesitation of the instincts, taxonomy begins to arise. This is a major and primal transformation, in which the instinct of natural man becomes the semiotics of cultural man. It is repeated, perhaps, in the psychological development of each human organism. At any rate, the process brings about the birth of that which is common and necessary to the systems of language and culture, and to all other systems; it accomplishes the nativity of signs, an accomplishment that makes mediation and, in a sense, art, possible: "Language does not enter into a world of accomplished objectives merely to give purely external and arbitrary signs or 'names' to individual given objects which are clearly delimited from one another; but it is itself a mediator in the formation of objects. In one sense it is the supreme denominator" (494).

8. See Claude Lévi-Strauss, *The Savage Mind*, trans. unacknowledged (Chicago, 1966), Chaps. 5 and 7.
9. Lévi-Strauss, *The Scope of Anthropology*, 32.

Writing, and all order one is led to say, begins with this hesitation, with this stammer in the presence of desire. The capacity to defer satisfaction implies a margin of differences and therefore the possibility not only of choice but of significant exchange. What is different, man may possess; what is the same must be foregone. To reverse this process—to gratify a desire that has been prohibited in the interest of social order—would be to efface that margin, to return man to his prior condition in a nature unmediated by rules or systems. "To speak in mathematical terms," Lévi-Strauss says, "incest is the 'limit' of reciprocity, i.e., the point at which it cancels itself out" (454). An act of incest, then, would free man of law—of any law, if this prohibition is the first and constituting one. Incest in this sense would be a cataclysm, a sort of epistemological apocalypse, or as John Irwin puts it a "suicidal return to the womb, the sexual reentry into Mother Death, an act that obliterates the differences between male and female, subject and object, conscious and unconscious, animate and inanimate."[10] In speaking of Pierre, Eric Sundquist makes much the same point. Pierre's "resolves," he says, "contradict one another irreconcilably, and every attempt to fall upon a valid origin dissolves as surely as his own fragmented identity."[11] Clearly, the result of such a violation must be that language, myth, kinship, whatever is born from the structuring principle of reciprocity and is subject to it, would return to an unmediated disorder. Man would discover, in this case, that his origin was nothing less than an absolute problematic, an incessant violence.

This analogy between language and kinship systems, which have their common origin under the constellation of signs, may explain why incest and the abuse of language are sometimes equated with one another. In some primitive tribes, Lévi-Strauss tells us, the "supreme sin" which unleashes "storm and tempest" (one thinks of Lear's relationship with Cordelia) "comprises a series of superficially incongruous acts . . . marriage with near kin; father and daughter or mother and son sleeping too close to one another; incorrect speech between kin; ill-considered conversation" (494).

10. John Irwin, *Doubling and Incest, Repetition and Revenge: A Speculative Reading of Faulkner* (Baltimore, 1975), 91.
11. Sundquist, *Home as Found*, 161.

Certain primitive prohibitions, he goes on, are classified as "a *mis-use of language,* and on this ground they are grouped together with the incest prohibition. . . . What does this mean, except that women themselves are treated as signs, which are *misused* when not put to the use reserved to signs, which is to be communicated?" (495–96).

Certainly the equation held for one of the reviewers of *Pierre,* who stressed this same relationship between a ravished language and an unspeakable sexual deviation. Melville, the reviewer charges,

> has done a very serious thing, a thing which not even unsoundness of intel-lect could excuse. He might have been mad to the very pinnacle of insanity; he might have torn our poor language into tatters, and made from the shreds a harlequin suit in which to play his tricks; he might have piled up word upon word, and adjective upon adjective, until he had made a pyra-mid of nonsense, which should last to the admiration of all men; he might have done all this and a great deal more, and we should not have com-plained. But when he dares to outrage every principle of virtue; when he strikes with an impious, though, happily, weak hand, at the very founda-tions of society, we feel it our duty to tear off the veil with which he has thought to soften the hideous features of the idea, and warn the public against the reception of such atrocious doctrines.[12]

In the main, *Pierre* was badly received. Even the reviewers who ad-mired the book drew attention to its mad excesses, and several specified, as Evert Duyckinck did in the *Literary World,* an equa-tion between "the horrors of an incestuous relationship" and the style of "a literary mare's nest . . . alone intelligible as an unin-telligibility." And nearly all the contemporary reviewers under-scored the novel's "befogged nature," its confused and enigmatical bluster, and its sheer nonsense: "Thought staggers through each page like one poisoned. Language is drunken and reeling."[13]

Clearly the style of the novel and its concern with the theme of incest disturbed reviewers who had no way of seeing a logical rela-tionship between language and a violation of this particular taboo. But in *The Scope of Anthropology,* Lévi-Strauss suggests a connec-tion between language and incest which may help to illuminate

12. Originally published in the *Whig Review,* this comment is quoted in the Hay-ford, Parker, and Tanselle edition of *Pierre,* 390.

13. Quoted in Hugh W. Hetherington, *Melville's Reviewers* (Chapel Hill, 1961), 231, 238.

Melville's deliberate excesses of language. In texts or myths which deal with incest, Lévi-Strauss points out, riddles—questions without answers, conundrums which are in effect a closure of communication—play an important part. The incestuous hero is typically called upon to unlock an impossible puzzle: but why? "Between the puzzle solution and incest there exists a relationship, not external and of fact, but internal and of reason. . . . Like the solved puzzle, incest brings together elements doomed to remain separate: the son marries the mother, the brother marries the sister, *in the same way in which the answer succeeds, against all expectations, in getting back to its question*" (38–39). The discovery of incest, he goes on, is always assimilated "to the solution of a living puzzle personified by the hero. . . . The audacious union of masked words or of consanguines unknown to themselves engenders decay and fermentation, the unchaining of natural forces." Such an audacious and forbidden union eradicates the function "which is fulfilled in society by the exchange of women in marriage and the exchange of words in conversation" (39). An act of incest, then, returns an absolute opposition, mediated by a principle of reciprocity, to licentious and nonsensical confusion. An ambiguous and enigmatical language would logically follow such a violation.[14]

So there is some reason to expect that *Pierre,* which deals so explicitly with incest, which relies so fully on the theme of the enigma, which strains expression to its limits, and which (hindsight tells us) comes just at the beginning of a major reorientation of knowledge, would manifest a special or unusual attitude toward language. We could fairly anticipate, if what Lévi-Strauss proposes is accurate, that *Pierre* might be a text in which the linguistic counterpart of the exchange structure undergoes a radical transformation. Putting aside the pronounced neologisms and hyperbolic figures of speech—pronounced even for Melville—the chief linguistic transformation in the novel is one of metaphor, language which incorporates kinship by locating analogies. Like that of all romantic writers, Melville's style is oriented primarily toward analogical relationships, which is really to say that his language, and that of his

14. *Cf.* Harari, "Exogamy and Incest," 1234.

age, reflects the transcendental bias of Western metaphysics. In romantic literature, metaphor is to language as incarnation is to myth: it is an annealing of the difference between object and essence, a crossing of the frontier between man and a beneficent supernatural. This principle of analogy was, Emerson said in "Swedenborg," "implied in all poetry, in allegory, in fable, in the use of emblem and in the structure of language."[15]

But nothing was so simple for Melville, whose style, though certainly based on a metaphoric principle, reverses the Emersonian vision. Emerson's language was a commentary on the belief that the universe was a transparent structure made luminous by metaphysical correspondences. To use language in this kind of cosmos is "to reconstitute the very order of the universe by the way in which words are linked together and arranged in space." Language and nature, moreover, are identical in this regard: they reciprocate with perfect symmetry, "for in this natural container, the world, adjacency is not an exterior relation between things, but the sign of a relationship, obscure though it may be. . . . upon the similitude that was the hidden reason for their propinquity is superimposed a resemblance that is the visible effect of that proximity."[16]

For Melville this code of resemblances was eclipsed, and he attacks the principle of analogy upon which the literature of metaphysics was predicated. "From the nineteenth century onward," Foucault points out in a passage that might well describe Melville's dilemma of language, "a profound historicity penetrates into the heart of things, isolates and defines them in their own coherence, imposes upon them the forms of order implied by the continuity of time. . . . language loses its privileged position and becomes . . . a historical form coherent with the density of its own past."[17] Language, that is to say, repudiates its own metaphoric bias, turns against the paradigm for which metaphoric style was the sign, and reduces to a debris the metaphysics with which Western literature had come to define itself as a sort of scripture.

15. Ralph Waldo Emerson, "Swedenborg; or, The Mystic," in *The Works of Ralph Waldo Emerson* (5 vols.; New York, 1904), II, 299.
16. Michel Foucault, *The Order of Things: An Archaeology of the Human Sciences*, trans. unacknowledged (New York, 1970), 38, 18.
17. *Ibid.*, xxiii.

Melville focuses this process with a series of images that emphasize the discontinuity to which his metaphor is now subject. Both visually and logically, this figurative language is a representation of ruin. A better way of putting it might be to say that Melville's style is inimical to signs, since the sign in both its aspects—as signifier and as signified—undergoes a perfectly intentional erosion, and the lesson of such a language becomes, one critic suggests, "how within a few decades in early nineteenth-century America there was formulated a set of responses to the central problem in contemporary semantic theory—how meaning is established when no 'absolute signified' can be located."[18] Images which depict origin, consecration, or apotheosis—images, for example, of temples, shrines, memorials or memory—are therefore especially useful to Melville, since they adumbrate man's capacity to produce signs that celebrate significance. The ruinous tendency of this agglomeration of signs is extremely important, for it illustrates not only an attitude toward iconic images but also an interpretation whose aim is not discourse, but silence.

It is difficult to offer a single example of this phenomenon, since Melville works, as usual, by a technique of clustering which is above all procedural. The image introduced early in the novel of the ruined city of Palmyra, for instance, cannot assume its full meaning until more specific and critical metaphors have been gathered together to provide a context. But it will serve as a beginning. Here Pierre ponders his position as "the only surnamed male Glendinning extant" (7) and exults in "the monopoly of glory in capping the fame-column, whose tall shaft had been erected by his noble sires" (8). The concept is clear: Pierre imagines a memorial to his family, and to the hierarchical values it represents, with himself at the peak of the ideal structure. Much is involved: the optimism of a national history, the sanctity of a pastoral estate and the tradition for which it stands, and, especially, the unbroken sequence of a genealogy whose source is ultimately a divine paternity. Pierre's grandfather, "grand old Pierre," is a "vast General," a hero of the founding revolution and the perfect disembodied essence of a pre-

18. Philip F. Gura, "Language and Meaning: An American Tradition," *American Literature*, LIII (1981), 20.

siding origin. But Melville moves at once to suggest, in a metaphor which will become more complex and more corrosive, a limit to the concept of origin:

> In all this, how unadmonished was our Pierre by that foreboding and prophetic lesson taught, not less by Palmyra's quarries, than by Palmyra's ruins. Among those ruins is a crumbling, uncompleted shaft, and some leagues off, ages ago left in the quarry, is the crumbling corresponding capital, also incomplete. These Time seized and spoiled; these Time crushed in the egg; and the proud stone that should have stood among the clouds, Time left abashed beneath the soil. Oh, what quenchless feud is this, that Time hath with the sons of Men! (8)

Here the architectural metaphor which Pierre's fancy uses to create a structure of the glorified self is negated by another voice which reduces the ideal of self, as well as the possibility of the metaphor, to zero. This counterimagery depends on fragmentation. The "crumbling, uncompleted shaft" is sundered from its "corresponding" capital precisely as metaphor falls short of suggesting a usable correspondence between the debris of monuments and a precise meaning for "Time." The motif of this ruin—the "capital" that is never joined with its corresponding shaft to make a finished column, in support of some significance—indicates the real problematic of language in this passage. More than a word but less than a metaphor, a signified not wholly quarried from this intransigent language or joined to an image, though capitalized, the abstraction "Time" remains both critical and indistinct. It is beyond the grasp of this discourse; it is not realized through analogy and therefore does not help to establish any metaphorically privileged meaning for the text. The edifice which we briefly glimpse is Pierre's monument to a significant origin, but this gives way at once to the fallen city of Palmyra (whose chief deity was Bel—Pierre's diminutive endearment for his sister). The structure of his origin, then, is displaced by a reminiscence of ruin and the sister-goddess yet unknown. It can never be constituted as monument or as metaphor. It is prevented from coming into being *by* "Time," the ruinous idea which in spite of its "capital" is never given a corresponding literal and which, therefore, can never substitute idea for object. It remains ambiguous and corrosive, the enemy of meaning and desire:

Time is a violence deliberately called into the presence of this art in order to limit its power.

Outside of metaphor yet traversing to its center, a power bound to correspondence by rivalry—what is this opposite to desire, intention, meaning, metaphor? what marks the limit for Pierre? Melville calls it Time but cannot specify a metaphor with which we might understand it. We cannot see it but we may reason toward it by the logic of its effects. "Time," by virtue of the capital pun which is both laborious and subtle, reflects a capacity within language to hold its own potentially curative force in abeyance. Like the earlier puns, it is an instance of language working against itself. It ruins the intention or desire of metaphor and breaks the unity of the romantic sign into fragments. This energy appears, like so many of Melville's symbols, as a refusal of language to constitute a precise metaphoric dimension despite the rich metaphoric possibilities which language itself suggests. The Whale is a case in point; so is the mind of Amasa Delano. Here "Time" is idea without image, essence without object. Melville locates in this gesture of writing— the tumescence of the letter becoming a capital which both suggests and effaces some privileged meaning—the inability of language to go beyond the literal. Whatever the source of ruin and fragmentation, language cannot suggest it through a metaphor that points to something beyond itself, for it is exactly and only language which limits language—no Other, but the Same, which ruins the sign's exchange of idea for image. It is the word that falls short of the Word. We blunder if we expect "Time" to be incorporated in a metaphor. This is to look for evidence in the wrong place, like Le Strade or Monsieur G., who can only seek out a hidden that does not exist. It is not the kinship of language and essence but of language with itself that determines the problematic of this universe—not what is different, but what is the same; not the incarnation of spirit by Word, but the play of word and word, that makes language aptly conceived as a kind of incest, a relationship that finds meaning only in possibilities that have always been forbidden in the interests of exchange.

So although the effect of incest has not yet been established, its power is already felt in the implications of this language, in which the exchange of signifier and signified is inhibited by some unremittingly ambiguous and incestuous desire of the word to keep to itself. It is as if signification fell short of the sign's attempt to bracket an essence. The word *Time* itself signifies, of course, as does its *capital*. Certainly we recognize a lexical value in the representation. But this lies quite outside the possibility of metaphor. Time, in spite of its evident importance to a metaphoric sense of the paragraph, is split off from the images, disembodied. As an essence it is unknowable. We see the results of Time but there is no image to imply a logical or systematic affinity between what may be perceived and what animates it. Finally the image of ruins, which seems intended at first to teach us a "foreboding and prophetic lesson" about fate, leaves us stranded, shy of any metaphoric relation. This of course *is* the lesson, though we must learn it by what is missing; there is no "Cetology" here to mediate between the empirical world and essences. Metaphor is the object of its own native, powerfully corrosive force, and no signifying image is offered to specify the meaning of this force or to suggest that it is susceptible of being embodied in language. That forbidden idea has not yet been discovered by the text.

Perhaps this is always a problem of the representation of time. "The intuition of time itself cannot be empirical," Jacques Derrida has said, adding that the intuition of time "is a receiving that receives nothing."[19] But, he goes on, "every language fails to describe this . . . other than by metaphor, that is, by borrowing its concepts from the order of the objects of experience, an order this temporalization makes possible" (84). Yet metaphor fails here in exactly that task—the representation of its own function, which is the revelation of a timeless presence that takes shape in a "mode of temporality" and moves before us as a call to faith. This reluctance to complete or clarify an identity between the two terms which metaphor normally bridges—the objective realm of signifiers, and the signified order of essences—is characteristic of the language of *Pierre*. But the relationship between these orders is now effaced.

19. Jacques Derrida, *Speech and Phenomena*, trans. David B. Allison (Evanston, 1973), 83. Subsequent references will be given parenthetically in the text.

They are at odds and unmediated by metaphor. No exchange between them is possible. Signification can no longer create and
maintain a relationship between object and essence. Even when the
metaphor of ruins first introduced here reaches its fullest and richest
expression (in Enceladus, incestuous and "abased beneath the
soil," as we shall see), it remains the enigmatical debris of a structural principle. The text will offer no arbitration between these opposing terms. There is no voice, no language, no art which can anneal the disjunction. Metaphor can only intensify our sense of the
general ruin of language by having its own failure more widely applied against the institutions of culture.

But let us begin again with the easier assumption that romantic
metaphor is always an arc, that all romantic tropes based on analogy are paradigms of reciprocity: they begin with what may be empirically perceived or historically arranged, and arch over the dimensions of the objective world toward an ideal order whose value
they exchange with the horizontal sequences of history where they
begin. These metaphors bestow myth upon language just as exogamous exchange bestows culture upon nature. As Derrida says,
"Analogy within language is represented by an analogy between
language and something other than it." This means that when
metaphor is more than an ornament, when it has an ontological
status, it is the sign of an "immanent structure." Moreover, there is
"a certain systematic inseparability of the nature of metaphor from
the metaphysical chain which holds together the natures of discourse, utterance, noun, significance, sense, imitative representation, resemblance."[20] Metaphor thus reveals and constitutes structure. Romantic metaphor, Emersonian metaphor, is not rhetorical:
it is a hiero/glyph, or sacred sign; it imitates the generating voice of
God. As John Irwin has suggested, "An Emersonian essay is simply
the decipherment of a hieroglyph," because "the hieroglyphic emblem represents for a writer like Emerson a basic understanding of
the nature of the universe. . . . The sense of the people and things

20. Jacques Derrida, "White Mythology," trans. F. C. T. Moore, *New Literary History,* VI (1974), 14, 22, 37.

that Emerson writes about is that their real meanings are hidden, that to confront them is necessarily to involve oneself in a process of interpretation whereby the surface is penetrated and inner necessity revealed."[21]

The theme of incest, which Melville uses to deconstruct this divine/speaking, is particularly germane here. In the nineteenth-century novel as it was conventionally practiced, metaphor is associated with the progress of a sanctified desire. Erotic love leads man into communion with a universal structure of relationships. As Mrs. Stowe wrote in *Pink and White Tyranny* (a tired little novel of the sort which Melville satirizes in the early portions of *Pierre*), "When once marriage is made and consummated, it should be as fixed a fact as the laws of nature."[22] Marriage thus becomes a perfect coincidence of a metaphysical order: "The family state . . . is the aptest earthly illustration of the heavenly kingdom, and in it woman is its chief minister. . . . She is to rear all under her care to lay up treasures, not on earth, but in heaven."[23]

It is courtship and marriage—exogamous exchange—which effect in erotic affairs the transformation that metaphor effects in language. In the nineteenth-century novel, the process by which erotic relationships typically become signs of spiritual presence may also be understood as a transcending arc, a transformation of the domestic scene into a heavenly mansion (the image is characteristic in novels of the period) and a quickening of consciousness to perceive the fructifying analogies between flesh and spirit. Metaphor is itself a marriage, a coalescence of the phenomenal and noumenal orders of reality: and in nineteenth-century fiction, metaphoric language and erotic desire identically fulfill the terms of a metaphysical covenant. Marriage and metaphor—different versions of the same structural relationship between phenomena and noumena—define and validate the status of the text. They reconstitute an original relationship between man and a sacred origin, and in this sense are

21. John Irwin, *American Hieroglyphics: The Symbol of the Egyptian Hieroglyphics in the American Renaissance* (Baltimore, 1983), 13, 14.

22. Harriet Beecher Stowe, *Pink and White Tyranny* (Boston, 1871), 320.

23. Catherine Beecher and Harriet Beecher Stowe, *Principles of Domestic Science* (New York, 1870), 19.

hieroglyphic. Each is the sign—marriage erotic, metaphor linguistic—of a structure. The covenant which they represent guarantees reciprocity between two distinct orders of reality. This reciprocal principle transforms history into *eschaton,* and an irreconcilable difference, one that has existed since the Fall, is resolved.

Pierre believes that the discovery of just such a reciprocity has solved the mystery of his father's ambiguous representation in a vaguely licentious portrait which opposes "that pure, exalted idea of his father, which, in his soul, was based upon the known acknowledged facts of his father's life" (82). Countering the sanctified portrait officially accepted by the family, this darker one suggests a "subtly and evilly significant" (85) meaning at odds with the ideal father venerated by Pierre, and seems to conceal an "essence" oddly distinct from that "dear perfect father" (19) he has been taught to imitate. It is his illegitimate half sister Isabel whose sudden appearance explains the portrait's mysterious glance and opens the possibility of a metaphysical correspondence between the ideal and a troubling real to Pierre. Isabel seems at first to explain the contrast in paternal moods previously held unaccountable: the myth of the perfect father on the one hand, and on the other the historical father, capable of sin, merge in what Pierre first imagines to be a celebration of man's dual nature, a confirmation of the body's twinship with spirit. The divine father invests and transcends the earthly father; myth informs history, divinity transforms humanity. After all, Pierre naïvely imagines, he is himself the legitimate heir of a perfect (though lost) sire: his father's marriage had redeemed this youthful transgression; the choice for kinship secures his promiscuous desire. This visionary interpretation of the portrait effects (though only for the moment) a coalescence of object and essence:

> By irresistible intuitions, all that had been inexplicably mysterious to him in the portrait, and all that had been inexplicably familiar in the fact, most magically these now coincided. . . . by some ineffable correlativeness, they reciprocally identified each other, and, as it were, melted into each other, and thus interpenetratingly uniting, presented lineaments of an added supernaturalness.
>
> On all sides, the physical world of solid objects now slidingly displaced itself from around him, and he floated into an ether of visions. (85)

But as Melville will discover (and elaborate later on in *The Piazza Tales*), such an interpenetration of object and essence is only an enchantment. His novel has already begun with a deconstructing parody of sentimental fiction, the ossified literary tradition which joined phenomenal and noumenal reality in a symbolic marriage; and it goes on similarly to attack Emersonian transcendentalism. In short order, Melville moves to replace these two versions of an optimistic universe with a new epistemology based not on reciprocal exchange but on dispersion. Pierre's inability to defer his desire for his sister means that the priority of kinship relations has become malleable under the heat of his passion. Mother is sister; son is brother; sister becomes wife; lover becomes cousin; cousin becomes deadly enemy. The theme of incest marks the fatal tendency of his imagination to transgress the interdict that creates a structured universe.

This transgression signals other important transformations. The theme of incest is deliberately used by Melville to permute the idea of the text and the myth of divine origin on which writing had previously been based. The discovery of his illegitimate sister confuses Pierre's faith in paternal rectitude and its analogue, the divine sanctity which had been the foundation of an era's faith. Once the heir of a pastoral tradition which opened onto an irreducible plenitude, Pierre, the representative of the romantic sensibility in decline, becomes Phaeton, doomed son of Helius (the paternal sun-god whose power he wishes to claim as his own); Hamlet, the heir displaced by an incestuous stepfather; and finally, and most importantly, Enceladus, the doubly incestuous Titan who storms heaven to claim his place at the head of the divine hierarchy.

It is the role of Enceladus that most fully expresses the collapse of relationships in the novel. His destructive resemblance to this ruined demigod comes to Pierre in another vision in which the world of objects, now all "artificial," "slid from him and [was] replaced by a baseless yet most imposing spectacle of natural scenery" (342). The discovery of this identity occurs as Pierre is struggling to complete his own novel, the text which he intends to supersede and negate all other texts, but which is, like the metaphors which Melville uses to undo languages, "committed to imperfection, even before it had come to any confirmed form or conclusion at all" (338).

> With distorted features, scarred and broken, and a black brow mocked by the upborne moss, Enceladus there subterraneously stood, fast frozen into the earth at the junction of the neck. . . . [an excavation] had bared good part of his mighty chest, and exposed his mutilated shoulders, and the stumps of his once audacious arms. . . .
>
> Old Titan's self was the son of incestuous Coelus and Terra, the son of incestuous Heaven and Earth. And Titan married his mother Terra, another and accumulatively incestuous match. And thereof Enceladus was one issue. So Enceladus was both the son and grandson of an incest; and even thus, there had been born from the organic blended heavenliness and earthliness of Pierre, another mixed, uncertain, heaven-aspiring, but still not wholly earth-emancipated mood; which again, by its terrestrial taint held down to its terrestrial mother, generated there the present doubly incestuous Enceladus within him; so that the present mood of Pierre—that reckless, sky-assaulting mood of his, was nevertheless on one side the grandson of the sky. For it is according to eternal fitness, that the precipitated Titan should still seek to regain his paternal birthright even by fierce escalade. (345, 347)

No doubt this resemblance to Enceladus is a metaphoric one. The analogy is complex and defines the most important aspects of Pierre's shattered imagination. Predicated on a punning translation from "Pierre" to "stone," however (Enceladus is one of the innumerable rocky masses near Saddle Meadows), it suggests a tendency of language to drift toward a dangerous repetition of the same rather than a capacity to transform nouns into essences. And at any rate the analogy is limited and determined by the contamination of incest, which questions the difference without which metaphor cannot exist. The most prominent mythic problem of the novel is portrayed here, the motif of the demigod which Pierre, like so many of Melville's heroes from Tommo to Billy Budd, finds in some aspect of his imagination. But what exactly is the achievement of this metaphor? What is Pierre when he has become the demigod? The god is not only ruined but the object of an archeology, and this (like the passage on Time) implies not only Pierre's failure but the loss of an original continuity between personality and myth. Enceladus has become a memorial to the quest for divinity, and as Jean Starobinski says, memorials are monuments of a lost significance.[24] The figure of Enceladus, and by association Pierre, represents an incapacity of the sign to celebrate an original relationship. Neither is free of the "terrestrial taint" which their incest has doubly determined; therefore, Pierre's identity with Enceladus cannot serve as a metaphoric transformation of object to essence. The metaphoric relationship stops at the point of a phenomenal or eventual correspondence, and does not bracket a metaphysical origin: though a grandson of Heaven, he is also the son of earth by an accumulated incest which ruins his quest for the heavenly purity he seeks to embody. What then can the metaphor express but the deflection of an original desire to find the irreducible essence for which it may unendingly and freely substitute its objective terms? Metaphor thus turns, in the face of this bankruptcy, to what remains as a sediment of its original quest: the resemblance between object and object, along the plane of historical time; and the rest is silence.

So Pierre, who has attempted to renew the purity of man's soul, and to insist that man may be a metaphor of God, now sees himself, in this final and self-consuming identification of man with a divine origin, as the soul eternally tainted and limited by its union with the flesh. He falls between an earthly claim which has been renounced and a heavenly birthright which can never be gained. Pierre discovers that the dream of an ideal origin, different from himself but which he might by the law of correspondences become, is only a repetition of the soul's birth from, and into, a crippling incest. He descends from his dream into a retrospection which he can never transcend. Though he does not know it, he has already fulfilled the terms of his mythic origin in his desire for the sister, Isabel, Bel (or Baal), twin and double of the destructive and polymorphous sun deity whose worship is a falling away from the paternal God of Israel. The myth he falls into is not the one offered by the New Testament theology which he naïvely hoped to verify in a Christly act of sacrifice. It is not heaven which he gains by his devotion to this

24. Jean Starobinski, *The Invention of Liberty*, trans. Bernard C. Swift (Geneva, 1964), 180.

enigmatical sphinx, or the light of grace which a marriage to Lucy Tartan would represent, but a universe unmediated by exchange. To take on the father's role is therefore not an apotheosis; it is to become the limited and unaided self, the self doubled by an incest: not the New Testament Christ, but Bellini's.

This is to reach the blank wall which Bartleby silently confronts. Pierre's imagination, and with it the romantic paradigm, is desacralized. He is imprisoned midway between the terms of the age's metaphor. "Time—the time that he himself is—cuts him off not only from the dawn from which he sprang but also from that other dawn promised him as still to come"; so Foucault describes man caught in "a discourse whose tension would keep separate the empirical and the transcendental, while being directed at both."[25] The description perfectly fixes Pierre at the point of his silence. Neither a god nor a reflection of deity, and not yet a man free of his desire for this irrecoverable and irreducible unity, Pierre is the fading emblem of his own writing and his own text: a cipher. "I am a nothing," he tells Isabel (274). He has used up his language.

Pierre's only heritage, and the only heritage of his art, is the ambiguous conflation he cannot escape, the incest which mutilates the soul and effaces the myth of divine origin and end. But more is destroyed than the myth of divine origin. The cataclysm has effects on language. The corruption of this dream taints all discourse which follows from its illusory transcendent rhetoric, and Melville repeats the deconstructing symbol in several different contexts in order to emphasize his point. The status of the text, any text, is in question now: "All the great books in the world are but the mutilated shadowings-forth of invisible and eternally unembodied images in the soul; so that they are but the mirrors, distortedly reflecting to us our own things; and never mind what the mirror may be, if we would see the object, we must look at the object itself, and not at its reflection" (284). This mutilation holds for all metaphysical inscriptions:

> While the countless tribes of common novels laboriously spin vails of mystery, only to complacently clear them up at last; and while the countless

25. Foucault, *The Order of Things*, 355, 320.

tribes of common drama do but repeat the same; yet the profounder emana-
tions of the human mind, intended to illustrate all that can be humanly
known of human life; these never unravel their own intricacies, and have no
proper endings; but in imperfect, unanticipated, and disappointing sequels
(as mutilated stumps), hurry to abrupt intermergings with the eternal tides
of time and fate. (141)

The image of mutilation also defines the history of Isabel, which
displaces Lucy's influence (identical at first to that of the "common
novels" of the day) and effaces the power of the sentimental novel
and its metaphysical paradigm. Isabel's bewildered memory "had
caused her continually to go aside from the straight line of her nar-
ration; and finally to end it in an abrupt and enigmatical obscurity"
(136). Her memory itself is sphinx-like, and the heroine, once like
Mary Scudder the transforming center of the novel's world, now
signifies an origin that is lost rather than regained. Ambiguous,
too, is the hero's most significant memory, his recollection of the
perfect father, the divine origin whose identity he wishes to assume
as his own:

There had long stood a shrine in the fresh-foliaged heart of Pierre, up to
which he had ascended by many tableted steps of remembrance. . . . this
sacred shrine seemed, and was indeed, a place for the celebration of a chas-
tened joy, rather than for any melancholy rites. . . . In this shrine, in this
niche of this pillar, stood the perfect marble form of his departed father;
without blemish, unclouded, snow-white, and serene. . . . Not to God had
Pierre ever gone in his heart, unless by ascending the steps of that shrine,
and so making it the vestibule of his abstractest religion. . . .
   Judge, then, how all-desolating and withering the blast, that for Pierre, in
one night, stripped his holiest shrine of all overlaid bloom, and buried the
mild statue of the saint beneath the prostrated ruins of the soul's temple itself. (68–69)

With the knowledge that the anguished and divine woman to
whom he is mysteriously attracted is actually his sister, Pierre's ruin
begins. Initially, Isabel suggests an evocative value beyond the object certainties which had constituted his innocence. "Hitherto I
have ever held but lightly," Pierre thinks to himself, "all stories
of ghostly mysticalness in man; my creed of this world leads me
to believe in visible, beautiful flesh, and audible breath. . . . But
now! . . . He felt that what he had always before considered the solid

land of veritable reality, was now being audaciously encroached upon by bannered armies of hooded phantoms, disembarking in his soul" (49). The clear light of grace which the sentimental heroine held out as a virtual certainty for fiction is displaced. "Priestess, wife . . . she ministers daily in holy works of household peace, and by faith and prayer and love redeems from grossness and earthliness the common toils and wants of life"; so Mrs. Stowe described the character which Lucy typifies, the "divine force" who is "ordained of God to keep the balance between the rude but absolute necessities of physical life and the higher sphere to which they must at length give place."[26]

The tone of sentimental fiction is confident and imperative. But now it is the more imperative riddle of Isabel that must be answered, though the answer to this enigmatic problem, forbidden to man's knowledge but not outside his grasp, destroys the order of his world. The text of the letter in which she announces her identity, irregular, "almost illegible" (64), inscribed as it seems to him in a mixture of blood and tears, calls forth an echo of Ahab's brilliant madness from Pierre: "From all idols, I tear all veils; henceforth I will see the hidden things, and live right out in my own hidden life!" (66). But what he discovers makes all relationships obsolete. The enigma of Isabel is solved. She is the father's issue and the sign of his double nature, both different from Pierre, and the same. She opens the true meaning of nature, which is only another enigma, another shadow "distortedly reflecting," a "wondrous suggestiveness . . . eternally incapable of being translated into words" (282). Every such doubling destroys another relationship and sets the soul more at odds with a manifold and unstructured universe. As Pierre admonishes Isabel, "Thy true heart foreknoweth not the myriad alliances and criss-crossings among mankind, the infinite entanglements of all social things, which forbid that one thread should fly the general fabric, on some new line of duty, without tearing itself and tearing others" (191). But how could she know? Her beginning lies outside this structure; she is a metaphor of violation. And the

---

26. Harriet Beecher Stowe, *The Minister's Wooing* (New York, 1859), 568; *The Pearl of Orr's Island* (Boston, 1896), 164.

rupture of social alliance which she is but cannot see, of course, is exactly what we might expect to happen in the event of incest, which effaces the original and originating law. So Pierre becomes, at the moment of this commitment whose full meaning is still dark to him, "profoundly sensible that his whole moral being was over-turned, and that for him the fair structure of the world must, in some then unknown way, be entirely rebuilded again, from the lowermost corner stone up" (87).

The bricolage is fated to fail. Ruin, fragmentation, the collapse of all structures whether erotic, aesthetic, or mythic, ensue from the incestuous desire, which Pierre discovers to be the inescap-able condition of his origin and of man's. The union of the soul's "mother the world, and its father the Deity" (296) represents not a perfecting exchange in the marriage of nature and the supernatural, but a violation of the first prohibition, as the figure of Enceladus makes clear. Desire does not translate the soul to a higher sphere of essences; it is the soul's dark limitation, a corruption which doubles and redoubles an original violation.

The grounds of transcendental metaphor are thus erased from language. Phaeton, half man and half god, cannot assume his di-vinity. His apotheosis is a vain dream. The chariot of the sun, arch-ing heaven in his weakening hands, nearly consumes all nature as it falls from its arc, and Pierre is forced to gaze "upon the charred landscape within him" (86). What he discovers is that man can never—in history or outside it—become present to himself as per-fect essence. Pierre is limited to the empirical real, to the debris of a universe not yet reassembled as a concept of the modern. The task of literary realism may be said to begin at this moment, when ro-manticism begins to die.

Pierre, then, is a text which turns language back upon itself, in order to discover the point at which man may recommence to think, and to write, free of the illusion of metaphorical affinities. This is part of what Foucault calls "the Romantic revolt against a discourse frozen in its own ritual pomp," but it is also a question-ing, a self-interrogation, which neutralizes the power of the roman-tic sign and makes a new discourse necessary and possible. Relationships are eroded, not established, by this endeavor, and what had been held constant and lucid by the doctrine of correspondences now suffers the dispersion first marked at Babel and repeated for every episteme. Melville provides a forewarning of this when Pierre, newly arrived from Saddle Meadows to the city, encounters an "indescribable disorder" of drunken voices "in English, French, Spanish, and Portuguese, interlarded now and then, with the foulest of all human lingoes, that dialect of sin and death, known as the Cant language." In this "combined babel" he hears "words and phrases unrepeatable in God's sunlight . . . syllables obscene and accursed" (240). Such is Pierre's condition from the moment he commits himself to an unspeakable desire. He is called upon to begin, in the embrace of a scandal, a radical dissociation; to make himself distinct from the hierarchy and inertia of a language whose structure had held for centuries to the same center; and to effect, in Foucault's words, the "manifestation of a language which has no other law than that of affirming—in opposition to all other forms of discourse—its own precipitous existence."[27]

This is not, of course, a language from which metaphor has disappeared absolutely. Metaphor remains; but its capacity to confer a structure is severely weakened. Metaphoric tropes are no longer a means of ascension to another order of reality, but a self-reflexive doubling, another kind of incest, which binds man to the world of objects and to the limits of the human organism. The nature of the sign itself changes for Melville. The energy which enables the sign to bracket noumena is petrified; it falls into silence. And its opposing energy—the burden of history which all signs must bear, the capacity for combinations and sequences—becomes dominant.

The metaphor which Melville uses as an example of this transformation is the ruined memorial, which we have already seen as the father's shattered temple, as the ruins of Palmyra, and, finally, as the temple of nature, "stark desolation; ruin, merciless and ceaseless, chills and gloom" (344). Nature has become a debris whose fragments may be permuted at will, so far does the influence of this decentering image extend: "Say what some poets will, Nature is not

27. Foucault, *The Order of Things*, 300.

so much her own ever-sweet interpreter, as the mere supplier of that cunning alphabet, whereby selecting and combining as he pleases, each man reads his own peculiar lesson according to his own peculiar mind and mood" (342). Here Pierre has reached the point to which incest returns man—the condition prior to prohibition and rule, in which discourse is merely mood and metaphysics has not yet come into being. The metaphor for nature stresses the thematics of enigma and ruin: "As among the rolling sea-like sands of Egypt, disordered rows of broken Sphinxes lead to the Cheopian pyramid itself; so this long acclivity was thickly strewn with enormous rocky masses, grotesque in shape, and with wonderful features on them, which seemed to express that slumbering intelligence visible in some recumbent beasts—beasts whose intelligence seems struck dumb in them by some sorrowful and inexplicable spell" (343). But the Egyptian images which so fascinated Melville, and which express the riddling mask of a nature prior to a constituting hermeneutics, have already been anticipated in the passage which sets once and for all the limits of metaphysical inquiry and presides so darkly over the entire novel. Here Melville describes the soul's interpretation of itself:

> The old mummy lies buried in cloth on cloth; it takes time to unwrap this Egyptian king. Yet now, forsooth, because Pierre began to see through the first superficiality of the world, he fondly weens he has come to the unlayered surface. But, far as any geologist has yet gone down into the world, it is found to consist of nothing but surface stratified on surface. To its axis, the world being nothing but superinduced superficies. By vast pains we mine into the pyramid; by horrible gropings we come to the central room; with joy we espy the sarcophagus; but we lift the lid—and no body is there!—appallingly vast as vacant is the soul of a man! (284–85)

"Hark ye yet again,—the little lower layer," Ahab had cautioned Starbuck in defining the quest and its essences. But this novel carries the quest deeper and farther than *Moby-Dick*, not to a mystery but to a terrible absence. "Sometimes," Ahab says of his quarry, "I think there's naught beyond." But the bulk of that symbol and its manifest power give the lie to his misgivings. If the whale does not answer Ahab's question, at least it does not fail to engage the possibility of an essence. What it incorporates is by no means clear, but something beyond the order of phenomena is always there, if always out of reach. In the central burial chamber of this memorial, however, and at the heart of the structuring metaphor, we encounter nothing—nothing but the silence of the sign, the silence which is the "only Voice of our God" (208). But what can one make of this sign which is a denial of signs—at least of the old signs, immured as Melville imagines in the empty place of the father? In reading such signs, Gilles Deleuze says, "We are not physicists or metaphysicians: we must be Egyptologists. . . . Everything exists in those obscure zones which we penetrate as into crypts, in order to decipher hieroglyphics and secret languages. The Egyptologist, in all things, is the man who undergoes an initiation—the apprentice."[28]

But Pierre, the apprentice, a son bound to a father's desire, can originate nothing, he is apprenticed only to the *métier* (the "mystery") of blankness—the vacant scene of authority and of authorship: the horror of desire, the silence of meaning. And once the voice of his God has thus fallen into the silence which baffles all discourse, there can no longer be any basis for the metaphoric marriage of object and essence practiced by Emerson and by sentimental fiction. In the literature of domestic sentiment, Scripture is a vital origin and referent for all language, "enchanted with a divine and living power," as Mrs. Stowe wrote, adding, "Let us treasure these old words, for as of old Jehovah chose to dwell in a tabernacle in the wilderness, and between the cherubim in the temple, so now he dwells in them."[29] This is the belief on which the analogical episteme is predicated, the belief that (as Foucault says) "below the language one is reading and deciphering, there runs the sovereignty of an original text."[30]

With the discovery that man's relationship to any such origin is not a matter of reciprocal exchange between two orders of reality, but is rather an incestuous violation of the principle of reciprocity, the capacity of metaphor to open language to metaphysical es-

28. Gilles Deleuze, *Proust and Signs,* trans. Richard Howard (New York, 1973), 91.
29. Harriet Beecher Stowe, *Oldtown Folks,* ed. Henry F. May (Cambridge, Mass., 1966), 133.
30. Foucault, *The Order of Things,* 41.

sences must fail. The prohibition against incest is, Lévi-Strauss insists, "the one preeminent and universal rule which assures culture's hold over nature" (24). A violation such as Pierre's breaks that hold, and from the hierarchy of culture we are returned to the rhythms of nature. But what if these rhythms are only another dream? what if nature is indeterminate, "superinduced superficies" (as Melville says) indifferent to "the modalities of relations" (as Lévi-Strauss says)? We are then no longer dwelling in a universe of rules, but in "the permanent expression of a desire for disorder, or rather counter-order" (491). Here both language and desire can lead the committed artist only to the creation of another kind of text in which desire and language focus together on "A brilliant perfect surface—to begin with at least." [31] But that language is the achievement of Henry James.

31. Henry James, *The Golden Bowl* (New York, 1909), 216, Vol. XXIV of *The New York Edition of Henry James,* 26 vols.

CHAPTER IV

Howells and the
Failure of Desire

Without, the deep night paused, gray, impenetrable. Did it hope that far angel-voices would break its breathless hush, as once on the fields of Judea, to usher in Christmas morn? A hush, in air, and earth, and sky, of waiting hope, of a promised joy. Down there in the farm window two human hearts had given the joy a name; the hope throbbed into being; the hearts touching each other beat in a slow, full chord of love as pure in God's eyes as the song the angels sang, and as sure a promise of the Christ that is to come.

—Rebecca Harding Davis,
Margret Howth (1862)

The Venetians have had a practical and strictly business-like way of arranging marriages from the earliest times.

—William Dean Howells,
Venetian Life (1866)

In 1861—just three years after *The Minister's Wooing* began to appear in the *Atlantic Monthly*— Rebecca Harding Davis published "Life in the Iron Mills" there. Mrs. Davis' story is now recognized as an early, if minor, instance of literary realism, which in some ways could well be said to epitomize the beginning of the new literary mode.[1] Its focus is industrial; it represents social consciousness and social reform; its concern is honestly the very specific damage done by immense, obscure forces generated by heartless capitalist appetites. This world might indeed be said to concede the fragmentation and horror of Melville's empty metaphors. Superficially these two texts in the *Atlantic* seem clearly to oppose one another: the iron mills (a figure for the unfeeling process that crushes the human spirit), the despair and squalor of the scene, death by suicide, the failure of desire to transcend hopelessness, all of these seem at the outset to put Mrs. Stowe's noumenal resolution into relief, and to begin by acting on Melville's exhaustion of the text.

The narrator of "Life in the Iron

1. See, for example, Bernard R. Bowen, Jr., "Realism in America," *Comparative Literature*, III (1951), 280–81; and Larzer Ziff, *The American 1890s: Life and Times of a Lost Generation* (New York, 1966), 174.

Mills," for example, says that the air of the town "stifles" her. The smoke from the foundries folds "sullenly," it "settles down in black, slimy pools on the muddy streets."[2] The atmosphere is "a foul vapor," the air "thick, clammy"; and when from her window she watches "the slow stream of human life creeping past," she sees "masses of men, with dull, besotted faces bent to the ground, sharpened here and there by pain or cunning; skin and muscle and flesh begrimed with smoke and ashes; stooping all night over boiling caldrons of metal, laired by day in dens of drunkenness and infamy; breathing from infancy to death an air saturated with fog and grease and soot, vileness for soul and body" (430). And to make her point unmistakable, she reports in her room "a little broken figure of an angel pointing upward from the mantelshelf; but even its wings are covered with smoke, dotted and black" (430).

The scene of Mrs. Davis' realism, then, seems clear enough: the "thousands of dull lives . . . vainly lived and lost," the filthy manufacturing town, and the mill, "a city of fires, that burned hot and fiercely in the night":

> Fire in every horrible form: pits of flame waving in the wind; liquid metal-flames writhing in tortuous streams through the sand; wide caldrons filled with boiling fire, over which bent ghastly wretches stirring the strange brewing; and through all, crowds of half-clad men, looking like revengeful ghosts in the red light, hurried, throwing masses of glittering fire. It was like a street in Hell. (433)

Down into this place—both text and context: her story is its atmosphere, she says (431)—she wishes to conduct the romantic reader of fiction, whom she addresses directly: "I want you to hide your disgust, take no heed to your clean clothes, and come right down with me—here, into the thickest of the fog and mud and foul effluvia. I want you to hear this story. . . . I want to make it a real thing to you . . . Egoist, or Pantheist, or Arminian, busy in making straight paths for your feet on the hills" (431).

Are we to be scandalized, then? made to stumble in the straight path, the transcendent and redemptory way of our reading? Is the

---

2. Rebecca Harding Davis, "Life in the Iron Mills," *Atlantic Monthly,* VII (April, 1861), 430–51. Subsequent references will be given parenthetically in the text.

broken angel a broken sign, like Melville's mutilated text, his shattered sentimental girl? But look again. This Hell and its creatures are
not lost to Heaven's gaze. Though "no one had ever taken the trouble
to read its faint signs," there is, "if one looked deeper into the heart
of things"—the heart!—and "down under all the vileness and
coarseness of . . . life . . . a groping passion for whatever was beautiful and pure . . . a vivid glow of beauty and of grace" (434). The
man Wolfe (ironically, named a beast) and Deborah, the wretched
girl who hopelessly loves him, provide the focus of desire in this
little story; and desire points the way out. What they respond to in
one another, and it is quite apart from any erotic feeling, allows the
text its elsewhere. Deborah watches him "bent over the furnace
with his iron pole" (435), but this image only displaces his sexual
desire onto the relentless demands of the mill. The celebration of
erotic desire, or its containment by metaphor, does not easily open
a way for grace. Mrs. Davis insists "I can paint nothing [but] the
outside outlines. . . . whatever muddy depth of soul-history lies
beneath you can read according to the eyes God has given you"
(434–35). We must look with the eyes of the soul; but when we do
we see not the metonymic fragment but an integrating vision, "not
like man's law, which seizes on one isolated fact, but like God's
judging angel, whose clear, sad eye saw all the countless cankering
days of this man's life" as well as this moment when "his soul
fainted in him" (435).

For Mrs. Davis it is man's life, not God, which is depleted; and
she sets out to find "a key-note to solve the darkest secrets of a
world gone wrong" (437). Hugh Wolfe differs from Pierre in his
powers of representation, his crude, striking skill as an artist, that
"had somehow given him a glimpse of another world than this"
(444). Nevertheless the "social riddle" (437) of this fetid place overwhelms him, the "mere drifting circumstances" of life put crime in
his way, something "commonplace enough," as she says (445); and
Wolfe loses his vision of "the incarnate Life, Love, the universal
Man" (444). Arrested, tried, convicted, sentenced, committed (the
process plays on the steps of Puritan conversion), he dies a suicide
in his cell instead of a bridegroom on the threshold of eternal life.
In the next cell Deborah, living in the prison near him, waits "in

dumb agony" as he fashions a blade to cut his wrists. Is it death, not life, that their love calibrates? They are kept apart; funeral takes the place of wedding, but it yields the same promise. Desire sees beyond the body. For Hugh, "a Voice may have spoken . . . from far-off Calvary" (449). As for Deborah, "slow, patient Christ-love" recuperates her "impure body and soul": then "with her eyes turned to hills higher and purer than those on which she lives,— dim and far off now, but to be reached some day," she waits "to meet there the love denied her here" (450). Finally the text presses its readers as it closes "through the broken clouds to the far East, where, in the flickering, nebulous crimson, God has set the promise of the Dawn" (451).

Nothing altered Mrs. Davis' commitment to the incarnate meaning of an apparently enigmatic and squalid reality. From *Margret Howth: A Story of To-Day* (1862), *Waiting For The Verdict* (1867), and *Dallas Galbraith* (1868) on to *Silhouettes of American Life* (1892) and *Frances Waldeaux* (1897) her trust in the metaphoric recuperation of exhausted souls sustained itself. Perhaps it is not necessary to rehearse the plots and paradigm of her fiction: what centers her text is what strengthens her characters, "an awful presence [that] walked with her always . . . step by step, and in that dread shadow she saw the things of life more justly." The paradigm remained a constant: an access to elsewhere, an alibi for desire. If it is true that desire associates to change, to a certain violence of personality (as Bersani suggests), it is also true that once articulated, desire tends not to require new forms of expression.[3] One could make the contrary case for de Sade, of course, but as a rule desire, having made its metaphors and its utterances, finds it difficult, perhaps dangerous, to escape their structure: once gratified, desire is not desire; it has become satisfaction. This may explain the violence that is necessary to a new desire: it is because two modes of desire confront one another: desire satisfied, sedimented, having lost its memory of change: and what appears to be its opposite, desire seeking its own signature. In any case, the codes of desire once

3. Rebecca Harding Davis, *Frances Waldeaux* (New York, 1897), 169; Leo Bersani, *A Future for Astyanax: Character and Desire in Literature* (Boston, 1976), 66.

formulated tend not to change. Thus the question of desire, and particularly its association with a theological meaning, raised a problem for the development of a new literary mode. The power of sentiment, of desire as the sign of a life beyond life and of the structure of reality itself, presided over literary language on through the second half of the nineteenth century, whether as paradigm or problematic: and Mrs. Davis' enterprise, reaching from the early sixties on to the end of the nineties, exactly illustrates the difficulty which a genuine motive to reorient the powers of literature found when it came to shifting the structure of the text.

William Dean Howells, among others, begins to succeed in this reorientation. And, one should say, until this anachronism is overcome by Howells and the other realists, realist texts—insofar as their language remains unable to keep desire free of metaphysical reference—must be incomplete. But what exactly is realism? It is not the spiritual resonance which Mrs. Davis provides as a release from the network of organized capital, nor is it merely her representation of that social and ideological complex. And until the literature of realism is free to represent its own desire it is scarcely a literature. Conventionally realism is known as a mimetic language.[4] It is "common" in the sense of "average, ordinary, normal, democratic," highly detailed, socially committed, the record of surfaces. It is believed to be positivistic, psychological, empirical.[5] One recent critic has called it "the attempt to guarantee that all representations are exact copies of the original," and, he goes on, "This demand for the lost object's return to presence is the repudiation of all representations, all substitutes, in favor of the thing itself."[6]

On the other hand, realistic novels (another writer urges) "ironically exploit the incongruity between appearances and essences; they are full of misunderstandings, isolation, the inadequacy of conventional signifiers. Realists thus are forced to supplement

4. Erich Auerbach, *Mimesis: The Representation of Reality in Western Literature,* trans. Willard Trask (Princeton, 1953).

5. Edwin H. Cady, *The Light of Common Day: Realism in American Fiction* (Bloomington, 1971), 5.

6. John P. McGowan, "*David Copperfield:*The Trial of Realism," *Nineteenth-Century Fiction,* XXXIV (1979), 8.

metonymic representation with other forms of signification."[7] This is true; the strict metonymy toward which the realist style tends (for whatever reason, according to whichever imperative) proves itself to be an inadequate literary language, because it lacks the capacity of the signified to provide a field of integration—for the sign, for meaning, for the text, for reality; and this is reflected in an emphasis on alienation, which is another way of expressing fragmentation. In other words, the themes of literature may well be something like the dreaming of its signs: what the sign needs, it seeks to express through its narrative.

So Marshall Brown argues convincingly that "realism can best be considered a structure of consciousness. It is a mode of cognition congenial to many nineteenth-century writers and differing from both the associative mode that dominated in the eighteenth century and the reconciliatory dialectic of the major romantics."[8] Since whatever else it is realism is signification, Brown seems right to understand it as an epistemological act, "an underlying type of semiosis" (233). Obviously enough, realism turns toward the language of direct speech, which is partly to say that it rejects any allegiance to the artificial models of belletristic writing which it associated with romanticism and sentimentalism. But the realists, including Howells, were more complex in their attitudes toward language than this observation suggests. It has been said that the style of the realists places its emphasis on nouns and verbs and weakens the act of modification,[9] and this is an important feature of the style, since it restricts realism to a scene whose horizon tends not to exceed the concrete attributes of ordinary perception; and it points to a relationship between language and the composition of knowledge, just as Brown correctly insists. Indeed this trait may be the most consequential property of the realist style: the language of realism intentionally conforms to the limitations imposed on con-

7. Catherine Gallagher, "The Failure of Realism: *Felix Holt*," *Nineteenth-Century Fiction*, XXXV (1980), 376.

8. Marshall Brown, "The Logic of Realism: A Hegelian Approach," *PMLA*, XCVI (1981), 233. Subsequent references will be given parenthetically in the text.

9. Harold C. Martin, "The Development of Style in Nineteenth-Century American Fiction," in *Style in Prose Fiction*, English Institute Essays, 1958 (New York, 1959), 131.

sciousness by impressions, recollections, and objects, and it verifies the circumference of this knowledge by exposing the inability of language to pass beyond the precincts of what may be immediately and directly experienced.[10]

But, Brown goes on to say, realism is also the record of "a tragic battleground where the active force of a free individual . . . always succumbs to the mastering contingencies of historical destiny" (236). Add his observation a little earlier that "realism developed into a central issue in mid-century precisely because the conception of reality had become increasingly problematic" (227), and the literary history of the nineteenth century becomes clear: realism develops out of and as a struggle to understand the nature of reality free of the imposition on inherited forms, outside the limitation which they demand and, even, the clarity they allow: the search for a new language, a new structure of knowing and expressing, away from the decrepit or corrupt place of fathers, toward a new mode of desire. What else is *Adventures of Huckleberry Finn?*

In fact most recent critics would agree, I think, that realism interests itself in something lost, in some difference which measures human perception and feeling and finds them increasingly isolated from a corresponding system of essences. And it chronicles the effects of this loss as it seeks compensation—new forms, metaphors whose structure is not already stipulated. Realism is a language obsessed by the failure of its fragments to find the endow-

10. A case against the success of realism is made by Gary Stephens in "Haunted Americana: The Endurance of American Realism," *Partisan Review,* I (1977), 71–84. But as it seems to me Stephens lingers so extensively on the "dullness" of realism that he overlooks its subtlety. *Cf.* Kenneth S. Lynn, *William Dean Howells: An American Life* (New York, 1971). Lynn's reading of (for example) the brilliant opening section of *A Modern Instance* makes a more consequential point. I wish to suggest that the formlessness of the realist text may reflect a necessary resistance to the implication of literary form, which follows Melville's idea that all forms and signs are already "mutilated." But *cf.* Joseph H. Gardner, "Howells: The 'Realist' as Dickensian," *Modern Fiction Studies,* XVI (1970), 323–43; George M. Spangler, "Moral Ambiguity in *A Modern Instance,*" *New England Quarterly,* XLVI (1973), 236–49; and Henry Nash Smith, *Democracy and the Novel: Popular Resistance to Classic American Writers* (New York, 1978), Chap. 5. Two remarkably helpful essays have surveyed Howells criticism in recent years: John W. Crowley, "Howells in the Seventies, Part I," and "Howells in the Seventies, Part II," *ESQ,* XXV (third and fourth quarters, 1979), 169–89, 235–53.

ment of an original design, by the inability of metonyms to express a fundamental principle of unity which could underwrite all meaning; at best, it is a language of energies remorselessly set free; and these symptoms are epitomized by its greatest thematic concern, the inability of desire to find and lose itself in its object—thus failing to transform objectivity into a realm of pure presence, free of dependency or change. But not least, realism is characteristically a stylistic reaction against the codes of language which attempted to claim this invisible presence and incarnate it in language—against, that is, the literature of romanticism, which possessed what the realist texts did not.

No one more clearly exemplifies the realist vision than Howells, who Henry James once said could write solely of what his "fleshly eyes" had seen.[11] Realist symbolism has been called "imploding."[12] Thus Howells' symbolic language, one of the best of his critics argues, refers "not outside the story to a metaphysical or psychological truth, but inside the story, to reinforce some meaning already in the frame of the narrative."[13] Howells' use of language is a demystification. For him, the literary language of romanticism is a corrupt form, one which assumes an ideal order that has receded into obsolescence. To say that literary realism is mimetic, in fact, is already to acknowledge that its language has shifted away from the expression of metaphysical correspondences to the reflection of that problematic world in which consciousness can create an order only out of its own history and experience. It aims, therefore, not to set up a metaphoric code which binds noumena and phenomena, but to represent as fully as possible the context of the empirical vision, to reflect the sequential order of history. Realism emphasizes the merely contiguous attributes of experience. It assembles the atoms of a world whose ordering system has been exploded, arranging them along a horizontal axis as a mosaic whose pattern conforms to a social design. William James used this image of a mosaic to describe the "radical empiricism" he opposed to the

11. Quoted by Everett Carter in *Howells and the Age of Realism* (Hamden, Conn., 1966), 110.
12. Cady, *The Light of Common Day*, 8.
13. Carter, *Howells and the Age of Realism*, 134.

post-Kantian idealism of, for example, Josiah Royce: "Empiricism," James said, "lays . . . stress upon the part, the element, the individual, and treats the whole as a collection and the universal as an abstraction. My description of things, accordingly, starts with the parts and makes of the whole a being of the second order. It is essentially a mosaic philosophy."[14] And, finally, it is important to remember that this philosophy and this language arise out of the deconstruction which Melville had carried on, and take as invalid the metaphysics that informed the imagination of the earlier nineteenth century.

In literary realism, then, language represents the facts and events of a narrative in such a way as to reflect the historical order which replaces the structure of language oriented toward transcendence. This language does not use metaphor to express the transformational power of subjective experience, which in sentimental fiction works to alter empirical perceptions by making them the signs of spiritual presence. The sentimental novel moves toward the celebration of marriage in order to represent a metaphysical conjunction. But the chief theme of William Dean Howells' first important novel, *A Modern Instance* (1882)—a novel that sets itself against the conventions of domestic sentiment, as we shall see—is divorce. And Howells' reluctance to assemble language metaphorically, a tendency he shared with the other American realists, suggests that it is not just the divorce of his two central characters that gives the novel a topic. Taken at a superficial level, divorce disintegrates the institution of marriage. But marriage in nineteenth-century American fiction had always been a moral and cosmological emblem, as it is in *The Minister's Wooing:* and the presence of divorce for the first time in the work of a major American novelist, one dedicated to the cause of literary realism, was a notable response to the conventions of his predecessors.

Howells' treatment of the erotic paradigm amounts to an attack on the cultural structure of which the sentimental marriage and the metaphorical style were models. The theme of divorce reflects the loss of structural relationships at all levels of culture. The collapse

14. William James, *Essays in Radical Empiricism* (New York, 1912), 41–42.

of the Hubbards' marriage, for example, is associated with the failed marriage of Marcia's parents, itself a symbolic union of her mother's helpless Puritanism with the mordant deism of Squire Gaylord. "The Squire has no religions," Bartley points out tactlessly, and though Mrs. Gaylord once had the characteristic sentimental hope "of converting him as women cherish who give themselves to men confirmed in drunkenness," her marriage teaches her that "in this great matter of his unbelief, her love was powerless."[15] She does not possess the language or control which are the properties of domestic saints. "Her life was silenced in every way," Howells tells us, and "the silence of her inward life subdued her manner, till now she seemed always to have come from some place on which a deep hush had newly fallen" (34). This silence of the inward life is also the silence of the metaphoric voice of language, muted by a culture's loss of faith.

The failure of this transformational language is associated with the failure of orthodox theology; and the theme of divorce in *A Modern Instance* represents not only a revision of the erotic paradigm of sentimental fiction, but also a departure from the doctrinal system which is replicated by the language of sentiment. In outlining his novel for *Scribner's Magazine,* Howells defined the question of divorce "as one of the few which are both great and simple. . . . I propose to take a couple who are up to a certain point about equally to blame for their misery; their love marriage falls into ruin through the undisciplined character of both."[16] The ruin of an institution is thus also the ruin of "character," of an inner moral quality: and in his novel Howells further identifies this "undisciplined character" as the result of Squire Gaylord's refusal to provide theological guidance for Marcia and, in a less explicit way, with Bartley's refusal to be educated in theology. Marcia at least recognizes her deficiency: "I think my worst trouble is that I've been left too free in everything," she says. "One mustn't be left too free. I've

15. David J. Nordlok *et al.* (eds.), *A Selected Edition of William Dean Howells* (16 vols.; Bloomington, 1977), X, 8. Subsequent references will be given parenthetically in the text.

16. Quoted in William M. Gibson, Introduction to William Dean Howells, *A Modern Instance,* ed. Gibson (Boston, 1957), vii.

never had anyone to control me, and now I can't control myself" (253). As for Bartley, he actively rejects the possibility of theological training. Orphaned early in life, when the benefactor who took him in "proposed to educate him for the ministry, with a view to his final use in missionary work, he revolted" (27). He and Marcia inhabit a world which does not offer the resources so clearly available to the characters of sentimental fiction, and this world is depicted in the novel by the town of Equity, Maine, where the narrative opens, of which Howells says "Religion there had largely ceased to be a fact of spiritual experience, and the visible church flourished on condition of providing for the social needs of the community" which had outgrown "the mood of . . . Puritanism" (24).

The failure of the marriage of Marcia and Bartley is thus the genetically consistent sign of their social context. It has its origin in the history of her parents' marriage and is the symptom of cultural disintegration, signifying both the tragic legacy of generation and the fluctuations of a historical order. This condition is doubled and redoubled in the other erotic relationships of the novel. Mr. and Mrs. Gaylord, Bartley and Hannah Morrison, Henry Bird and Hannah, the wretched desire of Ben Halleck for Marcia, even the marriage of Mr. and Mrs. Halleck, which cannot reconstitute its sanctified origin in their children: all these relationships are examples of the failure of the institution of marriage to consecrate experience and therefore to structure it. The extent to which American society itself is threatened by the rupture of divorce is stated by the conservative lawyer Atherton (who seems to express Howells' own views) and echoed by Halleck. And Halleck's own helpless desire for Marcia becomes the final subject of our interpretation. The "infamous laws" that permit a marriage to be dissolved, Atherton says, permit "scoundrels" to "lure women from their duty, ruin homes, and destroy society" (399), and Halleck bitterly repeats these opinions to Marcia: "You must keep [Bartley] bound to you, for fear some other woman, whose husband doesn't care for her, should let *him* go, too, and society be broken up, and civilization destroyed" (430). Divorce is the fracture of a ritual pattern, an explosion of order; it ruptures once and for all the ambiguous relationship between historical events and spiritual presence that Melville and Hawthorne had developed as the principal problem of their fiction, and decenters the institution which had once been the chief sign of a continuous mediation between man and God.[17]

A Modern Instance, then, is informed by Howells' sense of a failed theological structure, for which his motif is the institution of marriage; and this demystification of spiritual reality is apparent in his language, where the principle of metaphor is subordinate to the metonymic assembly of signs and events. The power to confer a hierarchy, which appears in language as metaphor and whose analogies in religion are Providence, grace, and ritual, is now absent from this world. When language ceases to structure experience, the intentionality of consciousness as well as nature is understood to originate within a closed system. Relationships are assumed to be temporal rather than teleological, as adjacencies rather than identities; relationships draw together the fragments of perceptions, the moments of a history which ceases to exist outside consciousness. "Nothing now exists," as J. Hillis Miller has said of Victorian fiction, "unless I think it." Due to the annihilation of God, "human subjectivity comes more and more to be experienced as a lack, as a devouring emptiness." Fiction in the nineteenth century both becomes and reflects "a pattern of incommensurate elements. These in their play of sameness and difference bring into existence a society which generates its own immanent basis for meaning."[18] Relationships are discovered without being consummated in the Word, and in the language of fiction such as this, the conversion of empirical facts into transcendental values becomes impossible.

Howells deals with this problem in ways that become subtle and complex. Early in the novel, after an evening at a church social, Bartley and Marcia share an episode of flirtation which, however

17. The contrary view is well stated by Ellen F. Wright in "Given Bartley, Given Marcia: A Reconsideration of Howells' *A Modern Instance*," *Texas Studies in Language and Literature* (Summer, 1981), 214–31; and see Lynn, *William Dean Howells*, 266–67, for suggestions that the institution of marriage is implicated generally by Howells' alarm at divorce. Lynn quotes a review by Horace Scudder: the novel is "a demonstration of a state of society of which the divorce laws are the index" (267).

18. J. Hillis Miller, *The Form of Victorian Fiction* (Notre Dame, 1968), 32–34.

apparently mild, is typical of their perilous irresponsibility. The house is silent as they talk, their conversation moving from one topic to another but gradually drawing toward a dangerous act of courtship which defines the problematic language of literary realism. Howells begins by limiting his representation of the characters to details: Marcia shows "a smooth, low forehead, lips and cheeks deeply red, a softly rounded chin touched with a faint dimple, and in turn a nose short and aquiline: her eyes were dark, and her dusky hair flowed crinkling above her fine black brows, and vanished down the curve of a lovely neck"; and Bartley is identified by "a yellow mustache, shadowing either side of his lip with a broad sweep, like a bird's wing; his chin, deep-cut below his mouth, failed to come strenuously forward; his cheeks were filled to an oval contour, and his face had otherwise the regularity common to Americans; his eyes, a clouded gray, heavy-lidded and long-lashed, were his most striking feature" (6). Perhaps "aquiline" and "flowed," together with the faint simile "like a bird's wing," temper the metonymy, but these tentative similarities only function as adjectives, underscoring physical details rather than opening the language to an idealization. Though Bartley's is clearly a weak face, there is nothing here that suggests the capacity of language to integrate a moral system, as there is in the description of sentimental characters.

Not only the physical surface of things but also inner, erotic experience is represented in this way. Bartley, for instance, makes a provocative gesture rather than committing himself to an intentional declaration of desire: as Marcia leans shivering toward the fire and reaches for her wrap, he says, "Allow my coat the pleasure" (7), closing its sleeves about her. Desire manifests itself in the attribute of an embrace, indirectly by the creation of an erotic context which evades the responsibility of anything so definite and unequivocal as a caress. Inner experience is indicated without being made explicitly present; it finds its language in a movement away from intersubjectivity rather than (as with sentimental fiction) toward it, in the projection of passion onto images that absorb desire and isolate it outside of metaphor. The degree to which the permutation and variation of conventions has become possible is now brilliantly represented by Howells. Just before leaving, Bartley extends to Marcia an invitation to go sleigh riding in his elegant cutter the next afternoon, and in the space of her hesitation, language breaks away from its structure to become the fragments of a vulnerable and unstable system. His request and her answer take place not in the immediacy of conversation but in the written formula of a letter, in the subversion of whose decorous and perfectly stipulated forms we observe the hierarchy of a conventional discourse ruptured and destroyed. A neurotic and violent language begins to take shape in the metonymic mode which has no recourse to, and indeed opposes, the metaphoric structure of language. Bartley and Marcia communicate here in a note which they pass back and forth between them.

"How ought I to begin? Dearest Miss Marcia, or just Dear Marcia: which is better?"

"You had better not put either—"

"But I must. . . . Dear Marcia: Will you go sleigh-riding with me tomorrow afternoon, at two o'clock sharp? Yours—yours? sincerely, or cordially, or affectionately, or what? . . . I think it had better be affectionately. . . ."

"And I think it had better be 'truly,'" protested the girl.

"'Truly' it shall be, then." . . . He wrote, "With unutterable devotion, yours truly, Bartley J. Hubbard," and read it aloud.

She leaned forward, and lightly caught it away from him, and made a feint of tearing it. He seized her hands. "Mr. Hubbard!" she cried. . . . "Let me go, please."

"On two conditions,—promise not to tear up my letter, and promise to answer it in writing."

She hesitated long, letting him hold her wrists. At last she said, "Well," and he released her wrists, on whose whiteness his clasp left red circles. She wrote a single word on the paper, and pushed it across the table to him. . . .

"This is very nice. But you haven't spelled it correctly. Anybody would say this was No, to look at it; and you meant to write Yes. Take the pencil in your hand, Miss Gaylord, and I will steady your trembling nerves, so that you can form the characters. . . ." He put the pencil into her fingers, and took her soft fist into his, and changed the word, while she submitted, helpless with her smothered laughter. "Now the address. Dear—"

"No, no!" she protested.

"Yes, yes! Dear Mr. Hubbard. There, that will do. Now the signature. Yours—"

"I won't write that. I won't, indeed!"

"Oh, yes, you will. You only think you won't. . . ."   (12–13)

We ought at once to notice the extent to which the epistolary conventions that Bartley is manipulating here tend to control desire. These conventions are prohibitive for a reason; they maintain a distance which permits emotions to be both expressed and kept in check. Like all conventions which arise out of paradox, they are a form of mediation, a means of transmitting or exchanging intentions without violating the social taboos controlling desire. But here the erotic game disintegrates these conventional prohibitions. It is played out with surrogates, its power represented by the hands of the lovers, which dance and struggle at the center of the passage, and by the phrases "Dear," "Yours," etc. The neutralized terms of erotic possession which open and close the letter are meant to delineate a special location where the force of desire may be mediated by a formal structure. But these forms are being fragmented, split off from their traditional usage and recharged with erotic implications, with an intention that is not a commitment. In the course of this letter they cease to be a mediation and become instead the signs of a potential violation. Desire is clearly on the verge of being freed from its prison in language, but it will not find expression in a metaphorical structure that might contain or transform its passionate energy: this novel will not grant a spiritual analogy to erotic desire. Desire is released rather than controlled, disengaged from the paradigm that formerly had made it the metaphoric replication of a structure.

Howells is using the traditional form of the letter to represent, without any sort of metaphoric imagery, a seduction and capitulation which indicates the disintegration not only of erotic conventions but also of language and of theology. In other words, the rupture of language is also an ontological event. Significantly, his style claims only the surface of experience as the text which it will reproduce and on which it will comment; but this is not to say that it is superficial. If the style does not produce the analogical structures of sentimental fiction, it nonetheless assembles according to a principle sufficiently complex to interest us. In the first place, it is important that Howells chose to represent the relationship between Bartley and Marcia by a written message that passes between them. In the epistolary novel, letters are typically introspective acts meant to communicate a private spiritual experience directly and absolutely through the use of a conventional form: they are the types of hierarchical language, the reassuring evidence of a structure. They neither demand nor permit the violence of desire, since they are based on the tacit agreement between author and recipient that language is a mediation. The fact that such letters are voluntary gives free access to the intention that motivates them, and interpretation thus becomes unnecessary. The letter is the consistent sign of an order, just as history and the novel are signs of Providence and the novel a sign of a *telos*.

Normally, the language of the letter is a highly crystallized social phenomenon, permitting desires to be exchanged without the intervention of an interlocutor. Its value is that it is an extremely stable mode of language, a text whose composition commits it to the custody of a form and an address. It has the privilege of remaining silent on all issues except those which it wishes to clarify and deliver. Like the novel, it stands for the writer's total system of language, and this is why we imagine him to be wholly responsible for it, why we value the written over the spoken word: the letter is the sign of a commitment; through it the author is responsible for the integrity of all language.

Howells' letter is different. It represents a disintegrating field of language which permits the instability against which epistolary conventions are designed to protect. In a way, it is a violation of sacred space, since the sanctity of its language is ruptured by the demands of Bartley, who overcomes Marcia's attempt to preserve her autonomy by means of the conventional forms of a decorous correspondence. He extorts a response from her and forces the transformation of her words into his; he breaks down language and rearranges it to gratify his desire. All the elaborate patterns that might control the lovers, which under the circumstances of sentimental fiction would open to analogous structures and represent them as the components of an orderly social and spiritual system, are reduced here to the simplest and most brutal elements of erotic language, to Yes and No, the response to his aggression of her propriety. No becomes Yes as Bartley preempts her power of language, changes her intention (if not her desire), appropriates even her sig-

nature, forcing her to respond literally as he dictates. It is this transformation, this obliteration of her language by his coercion, that
lets the reader know how arbitrary and unstable the system of language has become; and it is also what gives the scene its overtones
of violence and rape. The most vivid image of the passage gives a
sadomasochistic quality to their intercourse: he seizes, then re-
leases "her wrist on whose whiteness his clasp left red circles." Bartley leaves the sign of his passionate force on her blankness; the circle
of his clasp contains her freedom, her ability to use language independently. She becomes his prisoner; he has robbed her of her language and replaced it with his own.

With the loss of her language Marcia loses her ability to resist
the force of Bartley's. She cannot even recognize the soiled and
stolen speech which he uses in place of an original discourse. In
effect, she can do nothing now but say Yes to the violation of an
order which is summed up by the violation of language. Her desire
becomes an instance of the modern, the emblem of a culture whose
hierarchies have disappeared. The passionate violence associated
with her throughout the novel is a reflection of this initial act of
violence against her language. Her understanding is altogether enchanted by his inversion of the conventions of the letter, and Bartley moves now to create in the blank space of her consciousness a
history for himself and for their relationship. He speaks of the lecture they have just attended, the public act of language which takes
the place of the sermon. As he does with the private and interior
form of the letter, he adapts the speech in order to bring his own
context into being. Howells uses this lecture to suggest a problematical relationship between the act of language and an ethical standard. The address "was on the formation of character," and Bartley
uses it as the occasion of telling "of the processes by which he had
formed his own character" (13). There does not seem to be any
doubt that Howells is implying here a connection with the episode
just past, in which Bartley forcibly closes his hand over Marcia's so
that she can "form the characters" (12) of the language whose permutation he brings about: Bartley creates his own self by an appropriation of language.

For Bartley, in other words, history and morality have exactly the stability of language. He appropriates the lecture to celebrate his own "formation of character," to provide himself with a past, just as he forces Marcia to form the characters which are a self-gratifying affirmation of his unprincipled sexual overtures. Language, ethics, and history are equally malleable. If theology has degenerated into social amusement, language has similarly become the object and the agent of a pointless dalliance, and history a fluxional time which does no more than provide a setting for the creation of Bartley's own fictions.

Having succeeded in appropriating Marcia's language and transforming it into his own (an act that simultaneously makes possible the general disintegration of all structure), Bartley now offers in exchange the gift of a language to replace the one he has destroyed. He has used her to form the characters of a language which is powerless to resist his influence, and he now gives her back, in his concession of her influence over him—her formation of his character, the reconstitution of her mother's failed dream, as he makes her believe—precisely the fiction which she wishes to hear. This, however, is not an original idiom, but the tattered copy of an obsolete scripture. "'But of all the women I have known, Marcia,' he said, 'I believe you have had the strongest influence upon me. I believe you could make me do anything; but you have always influenced me for good; your influence upon me has been ennobling and elevating.'" In the face of this credo, Marcia loses for a moment the power of speech: "Her voice dissolved on her lips. They sat in silence." Into the space of a language destroyed by an unstructured desire moves the script of the defunct language of sentiment, that language whose voice is silenced by its own cliches. It is no wonder that at this moment, when the lamp begins to burn low, Howells moves (deliberately, one would prefer to imagine) directly away from the image of light, which in sentimental fiction is typically associated with the grace of the domestic saint. Though she offers to replace the lamp, Marcia does not move. "No, don't," Bartley says, "I must be going, too. Look at the wick, there, Marcia; it scarcely reaches the oil. In a little while it will not reach it, and the flame will die out. That is the way the ambition to be good and great will die out of me, when my life no longer draws its inspiration from your influence" (13–14).

Bartley's borrowings subvert the metaphoric language which constitutes a legitimate mediation between the self and its ideal significance. His use of metaphor, in fact, is only a measure of his corruption, and it serves the purpose of undercutting once and for all the power of analogy to express a structure. For Mrs. Stowe such an image would have been the center of a metaphoric text, the characteristic sign of a scriptural style. For Howells it is a means of dramatizing Bartley's exercise in derivation and bad faith; it refers not to a structure but to a history of writing, to a lost order which language cannot sustain, a hierarchy which has lost its privilege. This metaphor does not have the power to transform subjective experience; it only intensifies it without setting up a metaphysical dimension which desire may gain. By using this illusion to represent his emotion, Bartley reveals how fully his desire is a fiction. As he created his own idealized history from the text of the appropriated lecture, here he creates an erotic scenario; all language is a debris which he collects and uses to invent his own ego. Bartley constructs, with the metaphors of a formless reverie, corrupt myths of history and the self.

There are other indications that the order of culture is broken, that life has lost the authoritative structure with which romanticism began and which it later called into question. The theme of divorce treats the breaking of a taboo and is specifically related to the weakening of theological belief. One could read Marcia's elopement with Bartley as another instance of the deterioration of culture: the mechanisms which permit a woman to be given to a suitable husband have broken down, and this suggests that the kinship system no longer functions. The legal system that permits divorce is also presented as unstable and declining. Atherton's pronouncements on morality, though Howells shares a belief in them, take place in a prim and rather snobbish setting, which suggests a distance from the important issues of the novel; and both Bartley and Ben Halleck fail in their plans to become lawyers. Marcia's father, himself a man of law, not only fails to provide her with an inner sense of control, but breaks down in his legal defense of her. In filing a motion with the court which considers Bartley's suit for divorce, the Squire made "a futile attempt to prepare the paper; the pen flew out of his trembling hand. 'I can't write,' he said in despair" (440). The written forms of language are beyond him; and though his oratory draws listeners "in keen appreciation of his power" (443), his affecting presentation of "the record, unbroken and irrefragable" of Bartley's deceit is interrupted by Marcia's passionate withdrawal of her charges (445). Here the violence of her language seconds Bartley's scandalous desire: it ruptures the formal discourse of legal oratory and of the law itself, and her father collapses, paralyzed, bringing the structures of language, law, and the family into ruin with him. He returns with her to Equity, "the tremulous shadow of his former will," and watches feebly the ironic image of his granddaughter who "built houses with his lawbooks on the floor" (449).

Bartley's manipulation of language, which robs Marcia of a self and at the same time permits him to invent his own, is thus only one of a number of symptoms of cultural disintegration with which the novel provides us. *A Modern Instance* is a psychological study not only of divorce but also of related fragmentations which extend from consciousness to social institutions and myths, to law, marriage, and theology. The violent rupture of the conventions of the letter has the effect of seeming to initiate these others, since it is the first episode we witness, and indeed the demystification of language is so significant a fact that it may be inseparable from a cause. The problem of language is certainly the major one, not only for the novel but for the novelist: the contamination of language spreads through the entire narrative, touching all the institutions that language is called upon to express, and there is no structure, no dimension of metaphor, to restore the stability that is lost after the destruction of the letter. Bartley, in fact, regards all language—not simply Marcia's—as potentially his own. Twice he plagiarizes the anecdotes of his friend Kinney, and the second time Marcia, believing that Bartley's friend Mr. Ricker has written the article, refers to the act in explicit terms: "Why, how base! How shameful! That man shall never enter my doors again! Why, it's stealing!. . . Here's Mr. Kinney's life all written out! And when he said that he was going to keep it and write it out himself. That thief has stolen it! . . . I don't want you to have anything to do with such a *thief*! And I shall be proud to tell everybody that you've broken off with him *because* he was a thief" (318–19). In spite of the difference in tone, this is also true of Bartley's use of her language. No matter how Marcia may have intended finally to respond to his invitation, what she intended her No to mean or how she wanted him to interpret it, language once uttered must be countered only by another, reciprocal act of language. Otherwise the balance of the system will be destroyed, the discourse ruptured, and seduction will become rape. This is precisely what happens when Bartley alters her No to Yes. By denying the reciprocity on which language and all other structures are based, he does away with the conventions that mediate the irreconcilable opposites—nature and the supernatural, law and anarchy, chastity and sexuality—in the field of whose opposition culture takes its shape. This creates a scandal, the scandal of a violated perfect form: the institution of marriage, which protects, as Atherton says, against the destruction of the civilization of which marriage is both the model and the means of transmission.

This is the more ironic since Bartley has aspirations to be a "man of letters." He is a newspaperman who distorts the conventions of journalism just as he does those of the letter, turning them to his own ends without assuming responsibility for his own utterances. "I should cater to the lower class first," he tells his friend Ricker as they discuss the ideal newspaper; "I'd get my paper into such a shape that people of every kind and degree would have to say, no matter what particular objection was made to it, 'Yes, that's so; but it's the best *news*paper in the world, *and we can't* get along without it'" (263–64). The language of journalism, in his judgment, ought only to reflect the gossip of the day: even the religious news would be not only the religious intelligence "but the religious gossip, and the religious scandal" (263). The extent to which this attitude debases his language is clear several pages later, when Bartley meets a theater manager in a tavern. Asked what the substance of his latest piece is, the manager replies, with a sigh, "Legs, principally. . . . That's what the public wants. I give the public what it wants." These ideas "struck Bartley in their accordance with his own ideas of journalism" (267). Theater is metonymically reduced to "legs," journalism to gossip, the scandal of violated forms and conventions: and this metonymic representation of the drama emphasizes

Bartley's preference (scarcely a commitment) for the succession of merely contingent events. Indeed the Boston paper he works for is called the *Events*.

Finally it is through a newspaper—the chronicle of history at its most eventual—that Bartley sends his last message to Marcia. This is a public announcement, forwarded at his direction by a county clerk; the confusion of the letter and the newspaper, of the interior language of the soul and the public language of journalism, attempts in a sense to restore what was stolen from her and equally to reclaim what he lost in marrying her: the distance which language moves to close. His theft of language turned her No into a Yes; now in effect he is transforming Yes back into No with a letter of his own to which he expects no answer, which indeed he has caused to be sent not clearly to her but, as Halleck realizes, into a void: "This is the notice that the law requires she shall have to come and defend her cause," he says, "and it has been sent by the clerk of the court, there, to the address that villain must have given in the knowledge that it could reach her only by one chance in ten thousand" (406). If Bartley's behavior in the first instance amounts to an act of rape, this second letter is an act of perjury, a travesty of language. It is not reciprocity but denial; it reduces language to zero, society to its atoms. This is a language in arrears, like the letters which we see mixed with the "exchanges" from other newspapers that clutter Bartley's desk when he serves as editor of the *Equity Free Press*. These letters, Howells remarks,

> were mostly from young ladies, with whom he had corresponded. . . . They were not love-letters, but were of that sort which the laxness of our social life invites young people, who have met pleasantly, to exchange as long as they like without explicit intentions on either side: they commit the writers to nothing; they are commonly without result except in wasting time which is hardly worth saving. Every one who has lived the American life must have produced them in great numbers. (25)

"Every one who has lived the American life must have produced them in great numbers"—this is surely Howells' indictment of language and culture, the exercise which commits its writers to nothing. America's language becomes an arbitrary act whose correspondence with an ethical or moral structure is no more than an ambiguous accident. When Bartley, in his last theft of language, publishes as "news" a bit of spicy gossip about a citizen of Whited Sepulchre, Arizona, the outraged reader shoots him down. But this need not be the affirmation of a moral order. It may result simply from the serial coherence of history, which gives us the option of finding a concrete logic in events. The murder is not clearly presented as the long-deferred punishment of Bartley's violation of language; it is only "consequence or penalty, *as we choose to think it*" (451, italics mine).

The novel closes with an account of yet another letter, one which places language and morality in close proximity yet fails to define their relationship. It is written by Bartley's alter ego, Ben Halleck, to his friend Atherton. Halleck, after Marcia's refusal to press her case against Bartley, has entered the ministry and "returned to the faith which had been taught him almost before he could speak" (450), returned, that is, to the antique cultural structure that is doubled in language. It is not easy at this point in the narrative to trust the information that it gives us since the novel itself degenerates into gossip and other speculations; it "alleviates the history of tragic occurrences" (451); the text approaches, as it were, the condition of journalism as Bartley practices it. But some things seem to be clear nonetheless, though the novel demands a great deal of us at its conclusion—perhaps because Howells was having trouble in facing the universe that he had created. Halleck "freely granted that he had not reasoned back to his old faith; he had fled to it as to a city of refuge. . . . he rested in his inherited belief. He accepted everything; if he took one jot or tittle away from the Book, the curse of doubt was on him" (450). We may question the security of any "city of refuge," since it is in the very next paragraph that the novel reports Bartley's death in Whited Sepulchre, the city to which he has fled; and the motif of flight may apply also to Halleck's return to the shelter of an orthodox ministry, for the name "Whited Sepulchre" describes Bartley's character no more aptly than it does Ben's concealed passion for Marcia. Indeed the questioning of language, especially the language of the novel—itself a kind of letter by which the author corresponds with his reader—becomes an act by which the narrative undercuts its own form. Halleck's letter to Atherton is an example of a language that has grown so arbitrary that its structure disappears. Its permutations go to the heart of the system and break it into fragments. He asks the lawyer whether his desire for Marcia before the fact of her husband's death is not an offense "so great that nothing can atone for it" (452), and in two sentences that repeat an evocative homonym twice, creating the effect of a pun or perhaps only of an echo (in either case, of nothing more than an adjacency), he collapses the relationship of language and a moral standard on which the entire order of sentimental fiction is based. It is about his correspondence with Marcia:

> We *write* to each other, and there are times when it seems to me at last that I have the *right* to ask her to be my wife. The words give me a shock as I *write* them; and the things which I used to think reasons for my *right* rise up in witness against me. (452, italics mine)

This strange juxtaposition, which ambiguously associates the act of writing with an abstract ethical order, indicates, among other things, that the scripture of the Book which Halleck so wholly accepts cannot be translated into his own language. The problematical association of the verb *to write* and his confused sense of the noun *right* does not in any way replicate the legal and spiritual system which the language of Scripture incarnates. On the contrary, in spite of his orthodoxy we discover a disjunction that sunders the bond between metaphysics and the Word. Halleck's letter to Atherton, which is doubly important because it is a letter about writing letters—a kind of metalanguage—makes two opposing statements about the ability of writing to express emotion. At first, writing seems to turn Halleck toward a consecrated desire. The juxtaposition of *write* and *right* is initially reassuring:

> we write to each other . . . it seems . . . I have the right.

But in the very act of writing these words Halleck discovers that language destroys its own consecration:

> The words give me a shock as I write them. . . . reasons for my right rise up in witness against me.

His own language turns on him to subvert the process by which romantic writing discovered a justification for desire and thereby revealed the structure of which physical experience is a sign: his words witness against the scandal of a desire which their very presence has brought into being.

Language functions here as a mirror that doubles an image or a word. It separates the concrete dimension of "write" from the reflected, impalpable, and evasive dimension of what is "right." But the doubling is not metaphorical or structural. It is a fragmentation. The ethical potentiality of language is reduced to an attribute of the phoneme whose true value can now perhaps never be known, since it is lost in the neurotic self-reflexiveness of Halleck's vacillation. In his troubled and ambiguous motivation Howells represents the instability of a language which obscures its own vocabulary and themes. The appearance of an abstract or conceptual level of meaning is as complex a process as that by which the verb is transformed by an orthographic change into a noun, becoming in one sense a different word, yet in another sense remaining the same one. *Write* becomes *right* not by the metaphoric process in which language ascends the ladder of analogy. Here we move directly into the flux of a closed system which may be broken apart according to the pressure of a moment. What is operating on this language is the metonymic energy that splits the system up into its phonological, orthographic, and grammatical attributes. We have already seen this take place when forming the characters of a letter becomes the formation of character to which Bartley pretends. This unstructured language can no longer perform the function of mediation; it can only disintegrate as it reflects the oscillation of a desire that moves like the play of meanings within a sound. This condition is directly related to the weakening of the metaphoric principle, that mediating mode of language which draws together different words and orders of experience and makes them part of the same structure.

There is really only one point to which this fragmenting process of language can come, and Halleck himself brings us to it as he goes on to describe his courtship of Marcia. "I have never," he tells Atherton, "by word or deed, suffered her to know what was in my heart. . . . She is free, now; but am I free? Am I not rather bound by the past to perpetual silence?" (452). Halleck is the prisoner of the tendency of language; history and language alike impose their contingency on him, and he can only refuse to speak the words which might further corrupt the institution of marriage on which he imagines civilization to be based. Ben has become the mirror image of Bartley: the one betrays language, the other is betrayed by it, and both have been attracted by the same strangely passive but passionate woman to whom language can take only the most absolute of stances, coercion or silence.

Halleck's letter to Atherton thus asks a question that cannot be answered, poses a problem about the relationship of language and a metaphysical order that was opened when Bartley transformed No to Yes by his theft of language and thereby ruptured its structure. Atherton in fact does not believe that Ben can morally marry Bartley's widow because "his being in love with her when she was another man's wife is what he feels it to be,—an indelible stain" (453). This is not a theological assumption on Atherton's part, but a relativistic judgment based on Halleck's tendency to idealize experience. In Atherton's opinion the marriage would mean nothing short of disaster. "There might be redemption for another sort of man in such a marriage," he tells his wife, "but for Halleck there could only be loss,—deterioration,—lapse from the ideal." He does not recognize, apparently, that this is an ideal whose presence can never be recovered by language. "You're *not*," Atherton's wife asks him, "going to write that to him?" He replies with an abdication of language in the last words the novel speaks to the reader, thus cutting off the discourse which art has opened for us: "Atherton flung the letter upon the table, and drew a troubled sigh. 'Ah, I don't know! I don't know!'" (453).

The letter seems to serve Howells as an emblem for the problems of the novelist; it provides a means of demonstrating that desire and its language fail to draw even a merely social world together. It has been pointed out that Howells developed "a non-metaphoric style that has relatively little capacity for symbolizing the subjective modes of experience that his romantic predecessors commonly equate with truth."[19] When we consider that (as sentimental lan-

19. William C. Fischer, Jr., "William Dean Howells: Reverie and the Non-symbolic Aesthetic," *Nineteenth-Century Fiction*, XXV (1970), 5.

guage makes clear) this inner experience is commonly equated not only with truth but with a specifically metaphysical order of reality of which it is the sign, we begin to see that by refusing to allow language to provide a metaphoric dimension of desire, Howells shifts the style of realism away from the doubling of a structure to the reflection of a complex perceptual flux. Clearly much more than the erotic experience of courtship and marriage is questioned by the difficulties of Bartley and Ben Halleck to find within the resources of language some means of transcending the self and the world that perception absorbs. Their language consists entirely of a surface and a history; and it is not just Bartley whose use of language, lacking a metaphoric structure, fails to reveal presence. Language cannot serve as a means of mediation for Halleck or, for that matter, for Atherton, Marcia, or any of the other characters. Nor does it work that way for Howells, who once confessed that he himself was Bartley Hubbard.[20] Called upon to express desire in a way that might signify a dimension beyond the flesh, his language can only cast its reflections up against the boundaries of what is immediately before the senses.

20. In a letter to Brander Matthews, Howells remarked, "Yesterday I read a great part of *A Modern Instance,* and perceived that I had drawn Bartley Hubbard, the false scoundrel, from myself." Mildred Howells (ed.), *Life in Letters of William Dean Howells* (2 vols.; Garden City, 1928), II, 301.

CHAPTER V

Dreiser's Lost Language of the Heart

For here a woman was a woman, provided she was plump and rosy. Her mental characteristics or tendencies were of no particular import. It was her form, that mystic geometric formula which something has invented and which when contemplated by the eye of man inflames his passions.

—Dreiser, *Dawn*

When Ben Halleck, newly ordained, writes his friend Atherton seeking justification of his desire for Marcia Gaylord, he adds one more to the series of letters which organizes the novel—one which may indeed end the chain, for Atherton is not sure he can respond. The question seems to fall quite beyond the textual system of exchange. From the refuge of his belief "the lame young man," poor scandalized Halleck, appeals to the secular morality of an attorney. Theology seeks advice from law; a "backwoods church" and a "place on the Beverly shore," the "popular taste" of Aroostook County and the fashionable world of Boston, faith and reason, these polarized versions of New England understanding bracket the American romantic dilemma. On the matter of desire Halleck's conscience sheds "a fitful and uncertain light." He "no longer suffered himself to doubt," we are told; "if he took one jot or tittle away from the Book, the curse of doubt was on him."[1] If the master text is diluted, his reality falls under a shadow. The question of desire reveals the text's insufficiency—there is nothing in Halleck's Bible, however carefully he

1. David J. Nordlok *et al.* (eds.), *A Selected Edition of William Dean Howells* (16 vols.; Bloomington, 1977), X, 449–51.

sequesters it, which can resolve this doubt, or make his desire the sign of the regeneration he seeks.

Nor in Atherton's analysis. His wife Clara recognizes the need to substitute desire for law—"It isn't so much a question of what a man ought to have, as what he wants to have, in marrying, isn't it?"—but Atherton counters by insisting on the narrowest possible interpretation of feeling: Halleck's love, says Atherton, is only what he feels it to be, and that is "an indelible stain!"[2] But will this be his advice? that desire can be neither redeemed nor escaped? Though deeply troubled he does not know, cannot say.

So in spite of their mutual commitment to law, whether divine or civil, Halleck and Atherton cannot see by its light; and though they feel this dilemma as intensely as may be, they have no means of resolving it. Halleck is confused by his own desire, Atherton by his own analysis; and Clara's clarity is no help at all. With God's word or without it, the question of desire cannot be answered. Neither desire nor Scripture nor the letter as the text of desire can reconstitute the structure of marriage which Bartley and Marcia ruin; and for that matter Marcia herself, jealous, undisciplined, unstable—point for point her weaknesses match Bartley's—is not capable, as personality or as sign, of shifting the plane of the text away from its decline. As a sign of presence or regeneration, the institution of marriage is hopelessly damaged; so is the metaphor of woman; so is the whole redemptory apparatus of sentiment.

But the failed language of the heart—failed metaphor, failed recuperation of presence—continues to occupy American fiction as it seeks an integrated vision of reality. Canceling metaphor and its implications, canceling the structure of desire and the body of woman, canceling regeneration and language, restructuring itself to the discourse of fragments, realism thus found its problem focused by obsolete values which it had effaced and which immediately called for rejuvenation. As the matrix of grace, as a typical subject of the novel, desire has been generically part of fiction since its beginning. Indeed it was indispensably part of the fabric of American culture. "That religion which God requires," Jonathan Edwards observed,

2. *Ibid.*, 452–53.

". . . does not consist in weak, dull, and lifeless wouldings. . . . God, in his Word, greatly insists upon it, that we be in good earnest, fervent in spirit, and our hearts vigorously engaged in religion. . . . 'Tis such a fervent, vigorous engagedness of the heart in religion, that is the fruit of a real circumcision of the heart, or true regeneration, and that has the promise of life."[3] These holy affections—the Word's exhortation that zealous and joyful desire should willingly embrace God's intentions—center life for Edwards and illuminate its significance. And God's determinations for the world and His elect mirror a similar and self-reflexive joy in His own love for the origin of this manifold universe: "If there be many things supposed to be so made and appointed," Edwards says, "that, by a constant and eternal motion, they all tend to a certain centre; then it appears that he who made them, and is the cause of their motion, aimed at that centre; that term of their motion, to which they eternally tend, and are eternally, as it were, striving after. And if God be this centre; then God aimed at himself."[4]

This tendency to follow the heart's motive power toward a self-creating center is characteristic of the American literary mind from the beginning through much of the nineteenth century. God's Word urges the heart's desire for a new life; all nature follows this current. Scripture molds the heart to God's own pattern. Whatever his differences with Puritan theology, Emerson shared this ecstatic sense of a manifold creation unified by man's engagedness in an original analogy between flesh and spirit; and he shared, too, a ravishing desire for spiritual presence. In "Circles" he approvingly quotes Augustine, who "described the nature of God as a circle whose center was everywhere and its circumference nowhere," and in his essay "Love" he suggests how desire may bring man to an understanding of this centering godhead: "Beholding in many souls the traits of the divine beauty, and separating in each soul that which is divine from the taint which it has contracted in the world, the lover ascends to the highest beauty, to love and knowledge of Divinity."[5] Emerson and Edwards, despite their differences, be-

3. Jonathan Edwards, *Religious Affections,* ed. John E. Smith (New Haven, 1959), 99.

4. Jonathan Edwards, *A Dissertation Concerning the End for Which God Created the World,* ed. Edward Williams and Edward Parsons (New York, 1968), 531–32.

5. Ralph Waldo Emerson, "Love," in *The Works of Ralph Waldo Emerson* (5 vols.; New York, 1904), I, 119.

lieved in the capacity of desire to awaken man's sense of divine presence in nature, and thus to bring him to a centering and original relationship with essences.

The ramifications of this sort of language were emphasized (as Charles Feidelson has shown) by Horace Bushnell: "I discovered how language built on physical images is itself two stories high, and is, in fact, an outfit for a double range of uses. In one it is literal, naming so many roots, or facts of form; in the other it is figure, figure on figure, clean beyond the dictionaries, for whatever it can properly signify. . . . The second, third, and thirtieth senses of words—all but the physical first sense—belong to the empyrean, and are given, as we see in the prophets, to be inspired by." An organic relationship between phenomenal and noumenal reality is the basis of this language, which reflects the constituting principle shared by man's cognition and the physical world around him: "The external grammar of the creation answers to the internal grammar of the soul, and becomes its vehicle."[6]

This language is the agent as well as the double of man's desire for a center, indeed, is itself the process that fulfills his yearning for a manifold as well as a centering universe. "The most original book in the world is the Bible," Emerson had said; "this old collection of the ejaculations of love and dread, of the supreme desires and contritions of men . . . seems the alphabet of the nations."[7] Originating, centering, the sacred pre-text holds all acts of language to its perfect generative model. Desire seems almost a metaphor of language, as language is a metaphor of desire, in "Swedenborg": "In the plant, the eye or germinative point opens to a leaf, then to another leaf, with a power of transforming the leaf into radicle, stamen, pistil, petal, bract, sepal, or seed," and so on through the animal world to man where "nature recites her lesson once more in a higher mood. . . . Here again is the mystery of generation repeated. In the brain are male and female faculties; here is marriage, here is fruit. And there is no limit to this ascending scale, but series on series." The desire to replicate this order in language is made

6. Quoted in Charles Feidelson, *Symbolism and American Literature* (Chicago, 1953), 152, 153.

7. Stephen Whicher (ed.), *Selected Writings of Ralph Waldo Emerson* (Cambridge, Mass., 1957), 139–40.

clear in Emerson's journal, where he wrote, "Ah! that I could reach with my words the force of that rhetoric of things in which the Divine mind is conveyed to me, day by day, in what I call my life."[8] This metaphoric principle, this doctrine of gestating correspondences, draws matter and spirit together in an ecstatic union. "All writing is by the grace of God," Emerson also said, adding, "Give me initiative, spermatic, prophysying, man-making words."[9]

Melville was working on *Moby-Dick* at the same time that Bushnell was composing his treatise on language, however; and only twenty years after Emerson had called for "spermatic, prophysying, man-making words" Hawthorne had finished his last romantic study of fragments.

The realist novel is predicated on their fragmented language and lost desire—desire which wanders in the ruins of a language that once bound our passion to a healing logic. The favorite topic of Dr. Hopkins is "the last golden age of Time, the Marriage-Supper of the Lamb, when the purified Earth, like a repentant Psyche, shall be restored to the long-lost favor of a celestial Bridegroom, and glorified saints and angels shall walk familiarly as wedding guests among men." Emerson remarked much more brilliantly that "passion rebuilds the world for youth. It makes all things alive and significant." Though sentimentalized and maudlinized in many nineteenth-century novels, this structure is the same in fiction as in theology or philosophy. "Life is but a moment and love is immortal," Mary Scudder comes to realize, as she "seemed, in a shadowy trance, to feel herself and [James] past this mortal fane, far over on the shores of that other life, ascending with Christ, all-glorified, all tears wiped away, and with full permission to love and be loved forever."[10]

But desire in the realist novel, to be authentic, must avoid the illusion that experience and essence are metaphorically related. Desire that is free of this illusion arises in "a destructured world which has lost its meaning, a world in which things jut out like

8. Emerson, "Swedenborg," in *The Works of Emerson*, II, 293. Emerson, *Journals* (10 vols.; 1909–14), V, 376.

9. Whicher (ed.), *Selected Writings of Emerson*, 185–86.

10. Harriet Beecher Stowe, *The Minister's Wooing* (New York, 1859), 203–204, 540–41; Emerson, "Love," 115.

fragments of pure matter, like brute qualities."[11] And the style of this literary epoch, Roland Barthes has said, has "destroyed relationships in language and reduced discourse to words as static, things. This implies a reversal in our knowledge of Nature . . . initiates a discontinuous Nature, which is revealed only piecemeal. . . . Nature becomes a fragmented space, made of objects solitary and terrible, because the links between them are only potential. Nobody chooses for them a privileged meaning, or a particular use, or some service; nobody imposes a hierarchy on them, nobody reduces them to the manifestation of a mental behavior, or of an intention, of some evidence of tenderness, in short."[12] Once again language and desire may be seen as analogies of one another, though not as they were for Edwards or Emerson; from systematic metaphors of metaphysical essence, they have been transformed into systematic metaphors of man's alienation from divine affections.

Late in his life, according to both Robert Elias and F. O. Matthiessen, Theodore Dreiser came hesitatingly to express his desire for an Emersonian ideal of nature. Matthiessen suggests more accurately I think than Elias (to whom he is nonetheless greatly indebted) the ambivalence of this transcendentalist idea. In his earliest published work, including *Sister Carrie,* Dreiser unremittingly represented man and man's condition in terms that suggest Nietzsche's universe, a place of mendacious knowledge, "a mobile army of metaphors, metonymies, anthropomorphisms: in short, a sum of human relations which become poetically and rhetorically intensified, metamorphosed, adorned, and after long usage seems to a nation fixed, canonic, and binding; truths are illusions of which one has forgotten that they *are* illusions: worn-out metaphors which have become powerless to affect the senses: coins which have their obverse effaced and now are no longer of account as coins but merely as metal."[13] Matthiessen quotes a typical remark of Dreiser's: "As I see him the utterly infinitesimal individual

11. Jean-Paul Sartre, *Being and Nothingness,* trans. Hazel E. Barnes (New York, 1971), 371. Subsequent references will be given parenthetically in the text.

12. Roland Barthes, *Writing Degree Zero,* in his *Writing Degree Zero and Elements of Semiology,* trans. Annette Lavers and Colin Smith (Boston, 1970), 49–50.

13. D. Levy (ed.), *The Complete Works of Nietzsche,* trans. M. A. Mugge (12 vols.; London, 1911), XI, 180.

weaves among the mysteries a floss-like and wholly meaningless course—if course it be. In short I catch no meaning from all I have seen, and pass quite as I came, confused and dismayed."[14]

Sister Carrie had been published more than a quarter of a century before Dreiser wrote these words, yet they seem the best place to begin a study of language and desire in that novel, which initiates a century as well as a career. Language and desire in fact both signify something new by the time Dreiser had, with great difficulty, put his first novel into print. His reading of Herbert Spencer, Dreiser said, "nearly killed me, took every shred of belief away from me; showed me that I was a chemical atom in a whirl of unknown forces."[15] Desire too is a matter of "chemism" for Dreiser; man, he thought, "*is* a chemic animal, reacting constantly quite as chemical and physical bodies do to laws. . . . Life and the individual should be judged on their chemical and physical merits and not on some preconceived metaphysical, religious notion or dogma."[16] We might expect Dreiser's use of desire, then, and the language that expresses it, to conform to a pluralistic and uncentered universe, constituted by atoms in a "whirl" of energies.

Moreover this language and this desire provide no trace of an extra metaphysical presence beyond the representation of empirical experience. Dreiser's metaphors, when he does use them, do not indicate that language represents an experience of some order above language, which art signifies as it transcends the senses' limit. Dreiser's language, even his metaphoric language, allows no metaphysical elsewhere toward which the reader's desire might urge him. Indeed from the first sentence of *Sister Carrie* the atomistic aspect of the style, and of the new universe, is clear:

> When Caroline Meeber boarded the afternoon train for Chicago her total outfit consisted of a small trunk, which was checked in the baggage

14. Quoted by F. O. Matthiessen in *Dreiser* (New York, 1951), 235. Eliseo Vivas identifies the quotation as a passage from *Bookman* (September, 1928) in "Dreiser, an Inconsistent Mechanist," in Alfred Kazin and Charles Shapiro (eds.), *The Stature of Theodore Dreiser* (Bloomington, 1955), 241.

15. Quoted by W. A. Swanberg in *Dreiser* (New York, 1965), 60.

16. Quoted by Robert Elias in *Theodore Dreiser: Apostle of Nature* (Ithaca, 1970), 181.

car, a cheap imitation alligator skin satchel holding some minor details of the toilet, a small lunch in a paper box and a yellow leather snap purse, containing her ticket, a scrap of paper with her sister's address in Van Buren Street, and four dollars in money. It was in August, 1889. She was eighteen years of age, bright, timid, and full of the illusions of ignorance and youth.[17]

These images convey everything we need to know about Carrie and in fact most of what we are able to discover about her throughout the course of the novel. She is represented as a collection or succession of contiguous images whose meaning rests in their proximity to one another and in their constant repetition. She begins in transit; we encounter her just after the beginning of a journey whose terminus never comes clear. She carries only the signs of the traveler, four concrete images which substantially mark and limit her desire from beginning to end: clothes, food, money, and lodging. Moreover these images are all ephemeral—the lunch and the money are consumed almost at once, her sister's address is obsolete as soon as she moves into Drouet's ménage, and the cheap luggage, though an "imitation," is only a sign of a luxury she cannot have. All these will disappear when her lover purchases replacements for them. And the lover himself will soon enough be replaced. The details that present a concrete picture of Carrie are also the images that limit and analyze her character, and this limit, this analysis, is the fundamental assumption of literary realism: things are significant in themselves, not in their analogy to another order of things that is elsewhere than in man's history. Carrie is only what she appears to be, a figure in transit, a passive register of impressions and desires which are not sustained outside the senses. What is more, the images that define her disappear as she moves along, only to be repeated, made perhaps more elegant or conspicuous but never more significant: new clothes, richer foods, increasingly comfortable and affluent lodgings. Her characteristic movement through Dreiser's world is summed up by the ticket which she carries, a sign whose meaning is exhausted by the use to which it must be put. It is there to assure and signify passage, and becomes meaningless—

17. Theodore Dreiser, *Sister Carrie*, ed. John C. Berkey, Alice M. Winters, and James L. W. West III (New York, 1981), 3. Subsequent references will be given parenthetically in the text.

insignificant—once it has identified her as a passenger. It becomes effaced; it neither refers to her past nor points to any meaningful future. Like all the images that define her, its meaning arises out of its own obsolescence. Where a metaphor might compare, and thus detour, these details simply fade and reappear. Carrie's representation is never supplemented by an appropriation of anything outside language itself (with one exception, as we shall see).

An object herself, Carrie immediately becomes the focus of forces which continue to work on her throughout the novel. The sentimental coordinates that would have guided the heroine of one of Mrs. Stowe's novels remain behind her in Columbia City. With "a gush of tears . . . a touch in the throat . . . a pathetic sigh" (3) she gives up the reverie of sentiment. Only the merest iconographic fragments survive in the tears and the sigh. Leaving this context and its idealizing language behind, she enters a new dimension, one which Dreiser clarifies by using a metaphor which recalls and exhausts the reverie of an ideal world embodied in language:

> The city has its cunning wiles no less than the infinitely smaller and more human tempter. There are large forces which allure, with all the soulfulness of expression possible in the most cultured human. . . . Half the undoing of the unsophisticated and natural mind is accomplished by forces wholly superhuman. A blare of sound, a roar of life, a vast array of human hives appeal to the astonished senses in equivocal terms. Without a counselor at hand to whisper cautious interpretations, what falsehoods may not these things breathe into the unguarded ear! Unrecognized for what they are, their beauty, like music, too often relaxes, then weakens, then perverts the simpler human perceptions. (4)

This passage introduces a brief metaphoric construction which Dreiser must have found in some melodramatic seduction. But unlike the metonymic identity of Carrie, which is persistently reestablished in the novel's imagery, the suggestion of metaphor in this temptation is instantly deflated, along with the moral code toward which it momentarily detours. Desire for this false beauty does not kindle to a sign of man's unregeneracy. It fades only to reappear in another object. It is Drouet who commences this sequence of desired objects, and who checks the possibly metaphysical reference as well. To this chaste maiden, this innocent mind leaving the domestic hearth, the "human tempter" at once appears, summoned by the sentimental incantation to breathe corrupt lies into the "unguarded ear": "'That,' said a voice in her ear, 'is one of the prettiest little resorts in Wisconsin'" (4).

So much for the garden and its serpent. We have been asked by the overblown admonition to anticipate Satan whispering his cosmic lie to Eve. Dreiser invites us to expect the conventions and standards of the fiction to which *Sister Carrie* will in fact provide the antidote. But like all apparently moral coordinates in the text, this one disintegrates under the pressures of a writing that overthrows the sentimental and moral conventions of literature. Drouet is not a vile seducer, and his temptations are not the "falsehoods" which we have been led to expect by the allusion to a theological, epic, or melodramatic source; he speaks to the language of the senses: there is nothing else. But his words are only a reflection of desires already latent in Carrie, else she would not voluntarily be leaving "one of the prettiest little resorts in Wisconsin" for a new kind of life in Chicago. She becomes aware of "certain features out of the side of her eye. Flush, colorful cheeks, a light moustache, a grey fedora hat" (5) identify Drouet not as the enemy of virtue, since there is now no association (metaphoric or other) with supernatural values, no references to an absolute ethical system. Drouet is identified—once he actually appears in the context of this language—as a composite of signs, a character without depth. He is an individual type who stands for an entire class:

> His clothes were of an impressive character, the suit being cut of a striped and crossed pattern of brown wool, very popular at that time. It was what has since become known as a business suit. The low crotch of the vest revealed a stiff shirt bosom of white and pink stripes, surmounted by a high white collar about which was fastened a tie of distinct pattern. From his coat sleeves protruded a pair of linen cuffs of the same material as the shirt and fastened with large goldplate buttons set with the common yellow agates known as "cat's-eyes." His fingers bore several rings, one of the ever-enduring heavy seal, and from his vest dangled a neat gold watch chain from which was suspended the secret insignia of the Order of Elks. The whole suit was rather tight-fitting and was finished off with broad-soled tan shoes, highly polished, and the grey felt hat, then denominated "fedora," before mentioned. (5–6)

Surely what is being portrayed here is not the cunning tempter of nineteenth-century melodrama, much less his Miltonic prototype. This conventional association disappears almost as soon as Dreiser has suggested it, along with the fragments of the sentimental heart. And once this faint suggestion of a moral dimension to the fiction has been undercut by a language of pure surfaces (which is Dreiser's characteristic discourse), we begin to recognize that we are no longer in a world whose configurations derive from an origin outside of language. This is Drouet's function. He suggests the metaphor of an original temptation which then self-destructs; and the experiment may be endlessly repeated without any transforming effect. Drouet's banal observation to Carrie begins this process; it makes him no less than a masher but certainly no more than one either. He takes shape before her as he does before the reader, purely as a creation of the senses, an agglomeration of things which have no power to refer us outside of themselves. If anything is "revealed" here it is only details of clothing, and the most that is signified is Drouet's membership in a common fraternal organization. If man still has his totems, they are no longer mythic: the riddle of a "secret insignia," a sign containing a mystical reference, points only to a social banality. Our attention, with Carrie's (who has taken all this in with "her first glance"), is limited strictly to a sequence of images whose relation expresses nothing but the simplest empirical dimensions.

The limits beyond which this mode of language cannot go are indicated by its relationship to desire. Hurstwood addresses Carrie more skillfully than Drouet, affects her (or so she believes) more deeply, "exercised an influence over her sufficient almost to delude her into the belief that she was possessed of a lively passion for him" (205). The letters they exchange give strength and form to this feeling; but the origin of his desire for Carrie is not spontaneous, certainly not metaphysical. It is rather the expression of a self-reflexive process, repetitive but uncentering, which Dreiser suggests by describing Hurstwood's use of language:

> He was not literary by any means, but experience of the world and his growing affection gave him somewhat of a style. This he exercised at his office desk with perfect deliberation. . . .

... By the natural law which governs all effort, what he wrote reacted upon him. He began to feel those subtleties which he could find words to express. With every expression came increased conception. Those inmost breathings which there found words took hold upon him. He thought Carrie worthy of all the affection he could there express. (144)

The apparent freedom of Hurstwood's language to express his desire initiates a cycle in which feeling is endlessly repeated without transcending the limits of its exercise. By the self-reflexive gesture of his language, Hurstwood creates a hermetically sealed dimension in which desire is secretly stated. Within this dimension language and desire reflect one another as in a pair of facing mirrors. But this language is only the expression of a slightly richer desire whose superficial style Hurstwood has mastered just as Drouet has mastered an imitation of elegance. Hurstwood too derives; he cannot originate. The relationship of desire outside this special area of derivation is, and becomes more and more, problematic. The necessity for secrecy, for example, for social silence, suggests that this language is not free to make desire a means of transcendence. It is located in a kind of Sartrean nothingness; Hurstwood's language is what Sartre calls "only a perceptual reference of self to self, of the reflection to the reflecting, of the reflecting to the reflection" (54). He is in fact writing before the mirror of a derived self, and his desire turns inward rather than out toward Carrie. It is almost a soliloquy. Language and desire are a means of withdrawal, not of communion, for Hurstwood.

Carrie in turn never penetrates beyond this surface, which articulates her own desire to her. When she is with him she is always overcome by the fashion she associates with him: "Every hour the kaleidoscope of human affairs threw a new lustre upon something, and therewith it became for her the desired—the all. Another shift of the box and lo, some other had become the beautiful, the perfect" (145). This sums up the limits of Carrie's desire; her sympathy for the desolations of poverty, a side of her character that does not enter into her erotic attractiveness, escapes Hurstwood, who has never so much as "attempted to analyse the nature of his affection" (160). More than anything else, Hurstwood desires her desire, wishes to feel himself claimed as a necessary detail in Carrie's appropriation of an opulent universe. "What a thing it was," he thinks, "to have her love him, even if it be entangling!" (149). Carrie's desire for him would grant Hurstwood a value that he could otherwise not have. Taken by his family only as the unloved means to objects desired in a wholly impersonal way, Hurstwood is, in fact, as displaced as Carrie. "I want you to send the money I asked for at once," his wife writes, as Hurstwood reads "without a show of feeling"; "I need it to carry out my plans. You can stay away if you want to. It doesn't matter in the least" (235). In this relationship desire is inhuman; her letter is even colder than Bartley's; it focuses on objects to the perfect exclusion of personality. And, as Alexandre Kojève has pointed out, "In the relationship between man and woman . . . Desire is human only if one desires, not the body, but the Desire of the other; if he wants 'to possess' or 'to assimilate' the Desire taken as Desire—that is to say, if he wants to be 'desired' or 'loved,' or, rather, 'recognized' in his human value, in his reality as a human individual."[18] Hurstwood's dilemma is that he is himself incapable of anything but a derived expression of desire, and that Carrie is no more capable of a "human" desire than is his wife. Hurstwood makes, in effect, the same mistake in choosing his mistress that he has made in his choice of a wife; both indicate the flaw in his desire.

It remains, finally, for Ames to recognize and analyze the desire for Desire that makes Carrie's expression so enchanting to audiences and lovers. "The world is always struggling to express itself," Ames says, "to make clear its hopes and sorrows and give them voice. It is always seeking the means, and it will delight in the individual who can express these things for it"—and this is "the quality of that thing which your face represents," he assures her (485). Another version of the text of *Sister Carrie* makes this even more clear: "It's a thing the world likes to see," Ames says to her of her face, "because it's a natural expression of its longing. . . . Most people are not capable of voicing their feelings. They depend upon others. . . . One man expresses their desire for them in music, an-

---

18. Alexandre Kojève, *Introduction to the Reading of Hegel*, ed. Allan Bloom, trans. James H. Nichols, Jr. (New York, 1969), 6.

other one in poetry; another one in a play. Sometimes nature does it in a face—it makes the face representative of all desire. That's what has happened in your case."[19] For a moment, and only thanks to Ames, Carrie can glimpse her own desire represented in *Père Goriot,* no doubt by Rastignac, one of Balzac's "young and seeking aspirants" who so touched Dreiser.[20] The "novel was so strong, and Ames's mere commendation had so aroused her interest, that she caught nearly the full sympathetic significance of it. For the first time it was being borne in upon her how silly and worthless had been her earlier reading, as a whole" (495).

But Carrie is no Dreiser. "Becoming wearied, however, she yawned and came to the window, looking out upon the old unending procession of carriages rolling up Fifth Avenue." She cannot sustain Balzac's vision. "How sheepish men look when they fall, don't they?" her friend Lola observes as they watch "someone falling down" in the winter storm (495). So much for Pierre, so much for Ben Halleck; so much for scandal. Carrie responds "absently" just as Hurstwood, fallen himself to such brilliantly moving depths, has reached his "distinguished decision" (497) for suicide: in his "allotted room" he "reviewed nothing," hesitated, "stood there, hidden wholly in that kindness which is night. . . . 'What's the use,' he said wearily, as he stretched himself to rest" (499). His influence, like Drouet's, has become insignificant, and even at her immense and comfortable distance from his bleak death she is "the old, mournful Carrie—the desireful Carrie—unsatisfied" (487). Hers too are the "blind strivings of the human heart" (487), the merely repeated desires that can find "neither surfeit nor content."[21] No object of desire is significant; desire alone has meaning; and the meaning of this desire is that it cannot signify a final goal. Carrie at the end of the novel is no different from Carrie at the beginning, "responding with desire to everything most lovely in life, yet finding herself turned as by a wall."[22] She is drawn on and on by her

19. This version is from the Modern Library edition of *Sister Carrie* (New York, 1927), 537.

20. See Theodore Dreiser, *A Book About Myself* (New York, 1922), 411–12.

21. Modern Library edition of *Sister Carrie,* 557.

22. *Ibid.,* 555.

desire; but "Tomorrow it shall be on and further on, still leading, still alluring, until thought is not with you and heartaches are no more" (487).

The association of language and desire in *Sister Carrie*, then, signifies the dispersal of relationships. The rocking motion with which one version of the novel concludes carries her to a limit, brings her back again, begins once more and repeats the abbreviated arc that marks her captivity and signifies the limit set on her appetites. The metaphor is not a transcending figure; it is language cast up against that wall, thrown back, cast up again, until we begin to suspect that metaphor itself signifies her imprisonment within the restless oscillation of this language and this desire. This is why the images associated with Carrie disappear and re-form just as she replaces her wardrobe or her lodgings with more and more attractive ones. To use Sartre's phrase, this is the ensnarement of the body by the world. Carrie begins to "discover something like a *flesh* of objects. . . . From this point of view, desire is . . . engulfed in a body that is engulfed in the world" (368). Carrie is defined by objects which are never more than palpable. Like the language which gives them a momentary appearance, they only underscore the division of desire and metaphysics.

Throughout the novel metaphor is incapable of transcending this world to incarnate the noumenal structures which characterized romantic desire. There are times, however, when language, in order to represent problems which determine human behavior, shifts away from the metonymic axis. Any experience that is not sensory seems to bring metaphor with it:

> Her heart was troubled by a kind of terror. The fact that she was alone, away from home, rushing into a great sea of life and endeavor, began to tell. (10)

> Her mind was shaken loose from the little mooring of logic that it had . . . an anchorless, storm-beaten little craft which could do absolutely nothing but drift. (229)

> With her sister she was much alone, a lone figure in a tossing, thoughtless sea. (12)

But this metaphoric capacity, which expresses helpless isolation and dread, does no more than set the limits of Carrie's freedom—

as metaphor always does here. It is when the security of erotic attachment fades that metaphor becomes necessary; the more the
senses grasp, the less metaphor is needed. The final stages of Hurstwood's decay, for example, surely the most magnificent passages
in the novel, are represented virtually without any emphasis on
metaphor. Carrie's uncertainty, on the other hand, is typically
metaphoric.

This is worth investigating. When Carrie ceases to be an object
of desire, she ceases to exist in any real sense; and the language that
describes her opens to a vague metaphoric dimension. Though "not
enamoured of Drouet," Carrie "would have been utterly wretched in
her fear of not gaining his affection, of losing his interest, of being
swept away and left without an anchorage" (93). Dreiser repeats
the same metaphor so often that one begins to suspect he may well
have Locke's figurative language in mind—or more precisely, the relationship in Lockean epistemology between metaphor and the human understanding, which, in Locke, "finally begins to resemble a
small boat (to use one of Locke's own metaphors) in an unfathom-
able and threatening ocean." Such metaphors (and metaphors generally for Locke) "usually convey his ambivalent sense of man's rational powers. When used to portray limits they often suggest
despair."[23] The metaphor marking the limits of knowledge and
control for the great empiricist, then, may have been the perfect
one for the great realist to adopt: metaphor, the same metaphor in
fact, is associated with the movement from sensational knowledge
to man's tenuous suspicions of an experience beyond his empirical
perception. Metaphor, in other words, is the sign of a failed or limited knowledge.

An evident equation emerges for Carrie, in any case: loss of desire equals the appearance of metaphoric language. This is itself an
important reversal in fictive language, for nineteenth-century fiction had typically reserved its most important metaphors to represent a desire that expressed or at least interrogated the notion of
metaphysical presence. Dreiser thus inverts the paradigm of romantic texts. Without an erotic liaison the possibility of that desire

23. These observations on Locke are from an unpublished paper, "Locke's Use of
Metaphor," by Margaret Wooster.

which makes Carrie's own yearning for things feasible is negated, and her only measure of control dissipates. At such moments she experiences desire as an absence; and the possibility of a metaphysics, otherwise canceled by the prerogatives of sense, begins to haunt her. And at these moments Dreiser deliberately returns to a derived and obsolete language of origins. Carrie becomes the opposite of the sentimental heroine: losing desire, she loses history, while the sentimental woman, if she loses desire, risks losing a timeless plenitude.

The appearance of metaphor is thus a reminiscence in bad faith of another order of language, already reduced by Melville (in *The Confidence-Man*, for example, as well as in *Pierre*) to a fiction. Metaphor in Carrie's consciousness is a reference to something already lost to language—to the pastoral order she has left behind in Columbia City: she "half closed her eyes" during the first metaphoric instance I have quoted, "and tried to think it was nothing, that Columbia City was only a little way off" (10–11). But this metaphoric language, which returns as the sign of something lost, or rather as the sign of "nothing," no longer has the ability to constitute a unifying desire.

Dreiser seems to be aware of this when he treats the disintegration of Carrie's liaison with Drouet. Carrie "was getting into deep water. She was letting her few supports float away from her" (119). The instability of her erotic focus is reflected in an ephemeral language:

> People in general attach too much importance to words. They are under the illusion that talking effects great results. As a matter of fact, words are as a rule the shallowest portion of all the argument. They but dimly represent the great surging feelings and desires which lie behind. When the distraction of the tongue is removed, the heart listens.
>
> In this conversation she heard instead the voices of the things which he represented. How suave was the counsel of his appearance. How feelingly did his superior state speak for itself. The growing desire he felt for her lay upon her spirit as a gentle hand. She did not need to tremble at it because it was invisible—she did not need to worry over what other people would say—what she herself would say because it had no tangibility. She was being pleaded with, persuaded, led into denying old rights and assuming new ones, and yet there were no words to prove it. Such conversation as was indulged in held the same relationship to the actual mental enactments of

the twain that the low music of the orchestra does to the dramatic incident which it is used to color. (118)

Here language is displaced altogether; it is a "distraction" that only dimly represents a metaphoric "surging" which is prior in importance and power. And yet this great precedent desire fades even as it is named. The language that gives it form is clearly subordinate to "things," to the universe of signifiers which begins to impinge upon a willing Carrie from the moment she leaves her home and a traditional metaphoric vision behind. Though Dreiser describes Hurstwood's desire with a metaphor—it lay upon her spirit "as a gentle hand"—desire itself appropriates, as always in this novel, nothing more than a world of objects. In this conversation the language which speaks to Carrie of desire is that of "the things which [Hurstwood] represented." Nothing else is clearly before her. Desire "was invisible . . . had no tangibility," and "there were no words to prove" the erotic courtship.

Small wonder that this world is always struggling to express itself, that most people are not capable of voicing their feelings, when language disappears as soon as it is uttered. It is precisely as obsolescent as desire or as the signifiers that fill the space of Carrie's subjectivity. But at least she is free, as her language is, to make limitless substitutions within the restricted field of an empirical vision—within a vocabulary of things, so to speak, on which the claim of a grammar is the faintest and most rudimentary of traces. In spite of Dreiser's metaphors, which are in any case illusory, the experience of desire is entirely phenomenal. Dreiser's metaphor is lateral; it bonds objects along the plane of her greed, or Hurstwood's lust or despair. She desires signs, not feeling, not meaning; and the strength of her desire is that it needs no alibi, it requires nothing to provide a detour around the signifier that it seeks to claim.[24] Language only tints her experience, and for Carrie nothing remains of desire but the vague nostalgia for a sentiment that is all but forgotten. Language now becomes the reflection of a purely temporal reality; it is related only to itself, not to an order previ-

24. See Walter Benn Michaels, "*Sister Carrie*'s Popular Economy," *Critical Inquiry*, VII (1980), 373–90.

ously inscribed in nature. Like her ticket, it uses itself up. The play of this finite language is endless, its substitutions (like those of her desire) inexhaustible. It resembles the metaphors which describe her insecurity, or the echo of her home in Wisconsin—both memorials to an original reverie. It fades as it is used: "In presenting itself it becomes effaced; in being sounded it dies away."[25]

So the language of desire no longer functions to transform. It gathers and permutes a material world, but it cannot incarnate a spiritual order. This obsolescent desire is what mediates between Carrie and the world she wishes to enter, the walled city, and it is also the force that speaks against the fading conscience which unsuccessfully opposes the fulfillment of her longing. This is made clear in the dialogue which she carries on with herself just after having accepted Drouet as a lover:

> Here, then, was Carrie, established in a pleasant fashion, free of certain difficulties which most ominously confronted her, laden with many new ones which were of a mental order, and altogether so turned about in all of her earthly relationships that she might well have been a new and different individual. She looked into her glass and saw a prettier Carrie there than she had seen before; she looked into her mind, a mirror prepared of her own and the world's opinions, and saw a worse. Between these two images she wavered, hesitating which to believe. (89)

In this portrait the glass reflects Carrie framed by the physical objects Drouet has purchased as he has purchased her, objects which claim her desire as he does not: new clothes and a new apartment with a "good Brussels carpet on the floor, rich in dull red and lemon shades, and representing large jardinières filled with gorgeous, impossible flowers" (88). This is the fictive world soon to be epitomized by Jay Gatsby, with his gorgeous pink rag of a suit, his splendid cascading shirts, his swollen, gleaming auto, all the impossible metaphors with which he intends to recapture the lost ideal of desire. In Dreiser's novel the mental mirror and the carpet are both fictions, "impossible" figures of art framing a symbolic heroine, the heart of the Novel, whose "earthly relationships" are all reversed, like the images in the glass. Both figures suggest the extent to which representation risks putting itself in jeopardy: what

25. Jacques Derrida, *Speech and Phenomena*, trans. David B. Allison (Evanston, 1973), 154.

is portrayed becomes impossible by virtue of the metaphors which distort the world of objects, whether flowers in vases or the interiority of a young woman. The mirror of Carrie's mind is in such introspective moments "the labyrinth of ill-logic" (92). This is all that remains of Dr. Hopkins' theology, and it "represented the world, her past environment, habit, convention, in a confused way. With it, the voice of the people was truly the voice of God" (89). Like the images in the carpet, this representation is a false one. The mirror is a sign of the dangers of metaphoric writing, of the medium which tends to double the significance of its images and which, therefore, might seduce us into a detour around the implacable and dispiriting evidence of the senses. Metaphor is the alibi her desire no longer requires; it is the elsewhere of the image, the image caught in that mirror world and formlessly reflected back as an indictment. Its suggestion of Logos—"the voice of God"—implies an origin to which language can "in fact" never refer, just as the mirror can never validate the substance of the image which it represents. These ideal categories, these essences, are now only a confused debris. Carrie's mirror shows us an ideal dimension of language which has been lost, and what remains is a language that can reflect, at most, the fragments of the self.

The degree to which the language of desire has altered becomes clear, then, when we look at another passage from *The Minister's Wooing,* in which Mary Scudder stands "regarding the reflection of herself in the mirror":

> Nothing is capable of more ghostly effect than such a silent, lonely contemplation of that mysterious image of ourselves which seems to look out of an infinite depth in the mirror, as if it were our own soul beckoning to us visibly from unknown regions. The face . . . asks us mysterious questions, and troubles us with the suggestions of our relations to some dim unknown. The sad, blue eyes that gazed into Mary's had that look of . . . eyes made clairvoyant by "great and critical" sorrow. They seemed to say to her, "Fulfill thy mission; life is made for sacrifices; the flower must fall before the fruit can perfect itself." A vague shuddering of mystery gave intensity to her reverie. It seemed as if those mirror-depths were another world; she heard the far-off dashing of sea-green waves; she felt a yearning impulse towards that dead soul gone out into the infinite unknown.[26]

26. Stowe, *The Minister's Wooing,* 410–11.

This is a more complex image than Dreiser's, partly because the development of images into metaphors is a characteristic of Mrs. Stowe's language and not of his. Mrs. Stowe's use of the image is much closer to Hawthorne's, though in his style we may already see the difficulty of using this or any other symbol for spiritual reality. In "The Old Manse," "The Custom-House," *The House of the Seven Gables,* "Monsieur du Miroir" and elsewhere Hawthorne's difficulty in using the mirror as a symbol of access to a world of spiritual significance suggests the disjunction between the two orders of reality which his language attempted to close. Still, the mirror remained his favorite device for suggesting ideal or noumenal experience. A famous passage from the *Notebooks* testifies to this: "I am half convinced that the reflection is indeed the reality—the real thing which Nature imperfectly images to our grosser sense. At any rate, the disembodied shadow is nearest to the soul."[27] Mrs. Stowe is much more convinced. The "mysterious image" of the self reflected in Mary Scudder's mirror is like the soul made visible— this immanence is of course the purpose of figurative language for Mrs. Stowe—and expresses our relation to "some dim unknown" which is present in language and in desire. The identical image gives depth to Mary's experience as it does not for Carrie. The mirror, in spite of the fact that it isolates the self with itself in both instances, resonates in Mrs. Stowe's novel, draws consciousness toward "another world" and toward the state not only of Mary's soul but toward that of her lover's, whose salvation is in question.

It is perhaps because Mary is so capable of "self-renunciation," because her nature, like Christ's, is given to sacrifice and because she reflects his nature "as in a glass," that she can pass beyond the limitations of the moment or the event to "the good of being in general."[28] Nathaniel Emmons, the colleague of Lyman Beecher, puts it even more clearly: God's saints, he says, "they with unveiled faces, beholding as in a glass the glory of the Lord, are actually changed into the same image, from glory to glory, even as by the Spirit of the

27. William Charvat, Roy Harvey Pearce, and Claude Simpson (eds.), *The Centenary Edition of the Works of Nathaniel Hawthorne* (16 vols. to date; Columbus, 1962–   ), VIII, 360.

28. Stowe, *The Minister's Wooing,* 25, 354, 25.

Lord. God has given Christians a spiritual discerning of spiritual things."[29] What is especially important about Carrie, though, is that she can see no such thing. Her pleasure in the desired object only marks a single event along the axis of her experience. The mirror of her conscience, on the other hand, which is here presented on the verge of romantic silence, proposes an obsolete relationship that Carrie rejects. She opts instead for a structureless, fluxional mode of which her desire is an endless and a sourceless condition. Though she hesitates before her mirror, it is not for long. The images in that mirror of metaphor have no real existence and hence cannot serve her. Since they are not immediately present to the senses, they are a kind of non-sense. This absence may well empty Carrie and her mirror of meaning in several ways—economically and politically as well as spiritually: Carrie's "insatiability," Walter Michaels argues, leaves her perpetually diminished, always the sign of the promiscuous consumption which identifies American ideology: "Carrie's body, infinitely incomplete, is literary and economic, immaterial and material, the body of desire in capitalism."[30]

Dreiser, then, has used the image of the mirror to sunder the two orders of reality which Mrs. Stowe's mirror brought together. He presents us with the concrete image of Carrie's "glass" and with the mirror in her mind, the latter moribund and the former energized by the infinite repetitions of her desire. She is herself an image oscillating between these two reflecting surfaces, one of desire, which manifests an imperative present moment of the object, and the other of "her own and the world's opinions," the haunting conventional pieties that neither she nor Dreiser can trust. This schism concludes the central problematic of romantic style: the apparently inevitable drift of language away from that metaphoric union by which a manifold reality could be expressed within a single figure.

But to return again to our beginning: the unifying association of

29. Nathaniel Emmons, *The Works of Nathaniel Emmons* (6 vols.; Boston, 1842), I, Sermon 8, p. 108.
30. Walter Benn Michaels, "Fictitious Dealing: A Reply to Leo Bersani," *Critical Inquiry,* VIII (1981), 169. Also interesting is Bersani's response to Michaels' essay "*Sister Carrie*'s Popular Economy": Leo Bersani, "Rejoinder to Walter Benn Michaels," *Critical Inquiry,* VIII (1981), 158–64.

language and desire, lost in *Sister Carrie,* nonetheless functioned in our earlier literature to reconstitute or at the least interpret the metaphoric relationship between object and essence. In *The Minister's Wooing,* the effect of desire makes the theological language of Dr. Hopkins, that disciple of Edwards, more than dogmatic, and forces him to undergo in his own heart the emotional transformation without which his treatise would be sheerly rational. Affections for God, Edwards said, anneal the distinction "between a mere notional understanding, wherein the mind only beholds things in the exercise of a speculative faculty; and the sense of the heart, wherein the mind don't only speculate and behold, but relishes and feels." Here the "speculative faculty," the experience of the mirror (*speculum*) in which one sees what is "notional" or sensory, is doubled, indeed transformed, thanks to the heart's desire for God, which is signified and sealed in the sacrament of marriage. Thanks to the heart (as Edwards observed) "there is given to those that are regenerated, a new supernatural sense, that is as it were a certain divine spiritual taste, which is in its whole nature diverse from any former kinds of sensation in the mind. . . . that something is perceived by a true saint in the exercise of this new sense of mind, in spiritual and divine things, as entirely different from anything that is perceived in them by natural men." These speculations, these mirror-reflections, reveal (once divine grace opens the doubled sense of the reflected image) far more than the dimensions and substance of the object. They indicate a perfect metaphysical coalescence of covenanted men, "because holiness must be above all other things agreeable to holiness; for nothing can be more agreeable to any nature than itself; and so the holy nature of God and Christ, and the Word of God, and other divine things, must be above all other things agreeable to the holy nature that is in the saints."[31]

This is the annealing experience that brings about Mary Scudder's "hour of utterance" and fills her with the Logos of prayer.[32] Sentimental literature in fact typically explores the erotic paradigm as a means of bringing the world to its highest significance, uses

31. Edwards, *Religious Affections,* 272, 259–60, 261.
32. Stowe, *The Minister's Wooing,* 365.

desire (as we have seen) as the scene of significant utterance: the utterance of desire is simultaneous with the realization of a transcendent capacity, with the sense that the material world is a metaphor of spiritual presence and that language must therefore be consecrating. In Hawthorne and Melville this paradigm is tested and discovered to fail; and this failure of language and desire to transcend empirical limits occasions the romantic quest for the lost center.

So Carrie's consciousness and the language of Dreiser's novel can mirror nothing but the individual isolated among unrelated fragments. The mirror of Carrie's "average little conscience" briefly manages to state her "moral failure" to her, but the sense of hierarchy that it vaguely recalls is never a compelling presence in the novel, and at any rate is always disparaged by Dreiser's own commentary. "It was somewhat clear in utterance at first," he recalls, "but never wholly convincing. There was always an answer. . . . she was desireful. . . . The voice of want made answer for her" (90). The voice of want cancels the voice of God; desire effaces law. The loss of this utterance is also the loss of divine presence which American romantic fiction had explored. It corresponds to the use of the theme of desire to limit rather than transcend; Dreiser closes the equation.

But the loss is required by the oscillation of signs to be made good. The voice of the signified, that ghostly possession of reality which the plane of the mirror promises, and yet withholds, and still threatens, is about to return; it has already begun to make itself felt, obscurely and with great ambivalence but powerfully, in James, in his search for meaning among hints and anecdotes and rumors, among the spoils of presence. Carrie at least is free—alone and desiring but free of reflection, free of the beautiful subject's possession by the same ghostly meanings which haunt the mirrors at Bly.

CHAPTER VI

Henry James and the Art of Possession

The torment of possession is the greatest that man can suffer—the longest, for the demon never tires; the least understood, for the cause is invisible; the most dangerous, for it leads to the irreparable ruin of soul and body.

—Léon d'Alexis,
Traicté des Enérgumènes (1599)

Only the history of the symbolic function can allow us to understand the intellectual condition of man, in which the universe is never charged with sufficient meanings and in which the mind always has more meanings available than there are objects to which to relate them. Torn between these two systems of reference—the signifying and the signified—man asks magical thinking to provide him with a new system of references, within which the thus-far contradictory elements can be integrated.

—Claude Lévi-Strauss,
"The Sorcerer and His Magic"

The nineteenth-century division of signs displaces patterns and mysteries that were once assumed to be manifest in experience and in texts. Realist fiction ends by being torn between these two modes, which it fails to integrate. The development of literature in the fiction of Mrs. Stowe, Hawthorne, Melville, Howells, and Dreiser reflects the systematic shift away from the old unity of literary signs, and this is the result of a profound struggle, apparent as early as Mrs. Stowe's subtle restatement of Christian dogma, to realign the constituting elements of emotional and social textuality. Fiction thus resembles its own subjects, sensibilities abandoned by an image of unifying power. Pierre, Marcia Gaylord, and Carrie suffer a dread that haunts the world of forms. Largely that dread is an experience of their own desire, which fails to find a meaning for instinct. But a law by which desire can be sustained as a design is nonetheless imperative. Instinct, feeling, desire, the noumenal dimension of the sign: by any name this excluded value, however apparently menacing, requires to be admitted as an aspect of experience, supplementing reason and the density of events. For Mrs. Stowe it is reasserted as sentimental transformation: erotic desire is celebrated over a more logical submission to authority. But by the end of the century the power of sympathy had been disavowed. The impingement of noumena was understood to be a threat, a dangerous mystification of rational understanding.

So it is not only Carrie who is bereft, whose desire exhausts its own signs, who must wait to be possessed by something else. It is her world, Dreiser's and humankind's, where life relentlessly ends and begins again without ever becoming new or different. "The trouble with this attitude" (Dreiser says of Jennie Gerhardt's lover, the grossly materialistic Lester Kane) "was that it adjusted nothing, improved nothing, left everything to drift on toward an indefinite end."[1] Lester's deathbed reconciliation with Jennie seems, to be sure, the promise of something more; as she first thinks, it is "a testimony to their real union—their real spiritual compatability" (412), a "confession of spiritual if not material union" (423). But the richest context of symbols Dreiser can devise, the funeral mass of the Catholic church, fails to provide any signs sufficient to celebrate this brief illusion of meaning. Brilliant and solemn as it is, the ritual's moving splendor fails to console or transform. Jennie is "overawed and amazed, but no show of form colorful, impression imperial, could take away the sting of death, the sense of infinite loss" (428).

These forms and impressions are the limits of the order of signifiers: "Life in all its vagueness and uncertainty seemed typified by this scene" (427), and when Jennie reaches what is a much more intelligible place for Dreiser—the concourse of a great railway station, a terminal where origins and destinations may always be more simply and exactly specified, and where Lester becomes merely "a stiff" (430) to the workmen—she feels (just as Carrie had) "a wall, which divided her eternally from her beloved" (430); and she sees her future as Carrie does hers, "days and days in endless repetition, and then—?" (431).

The novel ends with a typical gesture; syntax too exhausts itself: "and then—?" The sequence of conjunction/adverb/dash/interro-

---

1. Theodore Dreiser, *Jennie Gerhardt* (New York, 1926), 415–16. Subsequent references will be given parenthetically in the text.

gation mark finds and goes to the limit of that wall. There is nothing of any clarity with which the conjunction might connect itself. The linkage promised by *and* dissolves into the ambiguous modifier *then,* into hesitation, into uncertainty. Such a literature as this, such a discourse of signs, can go no further toward expressing the shape of meaning. The question Dreiser reaches here is the limit of the realist sign, of the masterful signifier; it began to be posed at first by the romantic text, which broke the wholeness of literary discourse by scandalizing the regular cadence of signification.

What literature stands to gain by admitting that signs are scandalized is a genuine reconstitution of its values and form; but to concede this implies and leads to a thorough revision of fundamental values, which makes possible an integration of the contradictory (but mutually related) claims on human understanding. What it stands to lose, if it ignores the break in the sign's reciprocal cadence, is one aspect of significance, and thus the systematic exchange of values between objects and their meanings, between signifier and signified: by implication the whole principle of exchange, not to speak of the larger constituting field of cultural order (and the more narrow field of desire) in which symbolicity arises. This loss is nothing less than the possibility of a meaning which may be shared without being broken up, preserved as a system at the same time that it is bestowed as a value. In focusing their fiction so thoroughly on the claim of the signifier, the realists risked depriving literature altogether of its noumenal axis. Nevertheless their strategy was necessary if the overbalance toward feeling and sensibility, those old metaphors for the magic of grace, was to be corrected.

The paradox had to be resolved, and it was James more than any other realist who worked to supplement scandalized signs with noumenal possibility. He aimed specifically to clarify a dimension of meaning in the events and objects of desire. Reclaiming our lost share in an indivisible value is never far from the center of his fictive concern. In a sense this search for a lost or missing wholeness—a quest which always takes us along the axis of desire—is James's deepest and most pervasive subject, in Christopher Newman and Claire de Cintré, in Isabel Archer, in Maggie Verver and in Ralph Pendrel—everywhere in his fiction. But (to make a choice among many possibilities) the decade of the 1890s, especially the last five years of the nineteenth century, was an unusually interesting period in his revision of the realist aesthetic.

This was a time of marked artistic and personal insecurity for James. Leon Edel has shown how the fiasco of *Guy Domville* culminates his anxiety in 1895, and Walter Isle adds the importance of the nervous experiments with dramatic form that led up to James's disastrous humiliation. Indeed James had staked much on his effort; Kenneth Graham, who sees the nineties as the "most troubled decade in James's life as a writer," attributes the anxiety not only to the failure of the dramatic effort but also to the frustration of the deeper aesthetic and philosophical values that it represented. Undeniably this stress surfaced elsewhere in James's work. Charles Hoffman notes, in addition to the obsession with dramatic form, a parallel development in "the subtle handling of the theme of evil," beginning in the short fiction written between 1890 and 1894 and intensified in the maturer works of this period." And Edwin Bowden remarks a very agitated thematic emphasis (in the longer fiction written between 1881 and 1897) which "found its dramatization in the problem of the moral decision [made] by the individual," a sort of moral decision which is especially vexed, moreover, because it is "seldom a matter only of an ethical choice between right and wrong, but more often involves a choice between two ways of life, one offering some opportunity for a greater fulfillment of the human spirit, and the other offering eventual frustration and aridity."[2]

There is good evidence and some consensus, then, that James entered the closing years of the century in a state of troubled and experimental vision; bitterly shaken by his dramatic failure, but resolved nonetheless to revise and salvage his immense formal power; and determined to explore an influence that can accurately be termed threatening, and perhaps more precisely evil. These motifs

2. Leon Edel, *Henry James* (5 vols.; Philadelphia, 1953–72), IV, 83–95, 161, 168; Walter Isle, *Experiments in Form: Henry James's Novels, 1896–1901* (Cambridge, Mass., 1968), 77–119; Kenneth Graham, *Henry James: The Drama of Fulfillment* (Oxford, 1975), 127; Charles G. Hoffmann, *The Short Novels of Henry James* (New York, 1957), 52; Edwin Bowden, *The Themes of Henry James: A System of Observation Through the Visual Arts* (New Haven, 1956), 53.

convene; they provide the agenda for the work of the decade; and they are clear above all as they associate in the sensitive young women who fascinate James in texts like *What Maisie Knew, The Awkward Age,* "Maud-Evelyn," "The Turn of the Screw," and *The Spoils of Poynton.* These and other texts written during the last years of the century are organized around this cluster of interests, which leads James to an important development in the aesthetics of realism. The problem faced by his brilliant heroines, who bear no less than Mary Scudder the responsibility of making signs function, is exactly a question of desire: they face, all of them, the gulf between desiring and being desired, a desperate experience which represents the difference between finding or losing, once and for all, desire's place in a world of forms, a vantage from which one may recognize and share the power of the self.

The recuperation of form from engulfing horror; the anxieties of understanding and of action, on which the whole value of subjectivity is made to rest: these privileged aspects of his art, the relationship of which led James into his major phase, constellate in Fleda Vetch, the heroine of *Poynton,* whose struggle, James suggested, reveals "the method at the heart of the madness," the "splendid waste," of "clumsy Life." In Fleda we begin to see the great and powerful failure of an "opportunity for the sublime economy of art, which rescues, which saves, and hoards and 'banks,' investing and reinvesting these fruits of toil in wondrous useful 'works.'" Fleda reveals, she dramatizes, the central questions of James's art, questions which found the possibilities of order and relationship: "What are the signs for our guidance, what the primary laws for a saving selection, how do we place the beginnings of the wrong or the right deviation?"[3]

Fleda is the scene where the motive of these themes and strategies of signification may be known. Her life is a moment of the sign. Her agony causes us to see a deepening of the prominent metaphor which gathers all these various themes and which James repeatedly

---

3. Henry James, *The Spoils of Poynton* (New York, 1909), vi–vii, Vol. X of *The New York Edition of Henry James,* 26 vols. Subsequent references will be given parenthetically in the text.

used to focus his vision (and which by the way he shared with his brother William): possession, which for him is sometimes erotic, sometimes economic, sometimes demonic, but always the struggle of one force of will to objectify and use another.[4]

James's concept of possession emphasizes very special difficulties. Possession as the theme of a particular relationship—contradictory, self-opposing, yet fundamentally unified by its own ambivalence: this typically fascinated James (as, at roughly the same time, it did Freud).[5] In a fine insight Martha Banta suggests that the tensions causing this characteristic split in understanding are, for James, "as necessary as those that placed our universe on the rack."[6] This puts it very well; and I want to discuss this theme, which focuses a deeper question of literary language too, one that is figured in *The Spoils of Poynton*, where possession is a sign for noumenal claims on the empire of understanding.

Never doubt that possession was regarded as real from its beginning. In their time the symptoms of possession were "facts substantiated by evidence irrefragable according to the system of jurisprudence." Possession falls within knowledge and law. It implied, among other things, that "man was at all times exposed to the assaults of supernatural enemies, striving to lead him to sin, to torture his body with disease, or to afflict him with material damage"; it meant that "for good or evil, the barriers which divided the material from the spiritual world were slight, and intercourse between them was too frequent to excite incredulity."[7] Indeed this absolute difference explains the fury of possessive spirits. "Spirit lusts toward matter as matter towards spirit. The fallen angels are pure spirit. It is not enough for them. . . . A surge towards matter passes

4. See Martha Banta, *Henry James and the Occult: The Great Extension* (Bloomington, 1972), 88ff, 155. See also Gay Wilson Allen, *William James* (New York, 1967), 281–85; Henry James (ed.), *The Letters of William James* (2 vols.; Boston, 1920), II, 56–58.

5. See James Strachey (ed.), *The Standard Edition of the Complete Psychological Works of Sigmund Freud*, trans. James Strachey *et al.* (24 vols.; London, 1953–74), I, 242, XIX, 85, 86.

6. Banta, *Henry James and the Occult*, 85.

7. H. C. Lea, *A History of the Inquisition of the Middle Ages* (3 vols.; New York, 1958), III, 505, 383.

through the hierarchy of the abyss; they rush towards it; they speak the bodies of men and women; they desire to incarnate."[8] Considered in this way, possession clarifies as little else can the extent to which man has been the theater of metaphysics.

So one may say of possession what Foucault, writing of the age of reason, says of madness—that it was "not merely one of the possibilities afforded by the union of soul and body; it was not just one of the consequences of passion. Instituted by the unity of soul and body, [it] turned against that unity and once again put it in question. . . . [It] was one of those unities in which laws were compromised, perverted, distorted—thereby manifesting such unity as evident and established, but also as fragile and already doomed to destruction." Madness, Foucault goes on, "begins where the relation of man to truth is disturbed and darkened." Precisely: like possession in its periods, madness in the age of reason inflects human consciousness, whose unity is not thus dissolved but "fissured . . . along lines which do not abolish it, but divide it into arbitrary sectors."[9] Possession is the return of a discredited authority, the reassertion of a violent force which divides consciousness and poses an ambiguous dilemma. It requires the fullest civil and ecclesiastical apparatus to clarify the meaning of the poor wretch whose value is thus both problematic and immense. Like madness, possession brings about the mystification of signs; not only the body, which is the chief sign of possession, but also the universe that surrounds it and whose meaning the possessed body shockingly calls into question.

And that space of possession is much more than the body's or even the soul's. The space is textual: it implies everything that lies within the network of systematic differentiation, everything that man can achieve by the generative and violent exclusion of a ritual victim, that "mechanism which, in a single decisive movement, curtails reciprocal violence and imposes structure on the community." It is the theoretical geography of Culture, in other words; and it must also be understood as suddenly having become a space of

8. Charles Williams, *Witchcraft* (New York, 1959), 128.
9. Michel Foucault, *Madness and Civilization,* trans. Richard Howard (New York, 1967), 80.

radical transformation, of a profound reversal of order. It not only represents, it becomes and remains a critical condition in which "coherent thinking collapses and rational activities are abandoned" and must be ritually, even sacrificially reasserted.[10] Lévi-Strauss suggests the structurality of this event when he proposes that "the sorcerer-patient dyad incarnates for the group, in vivid and concrete fashion, an antagonism that is inherent in all thought but that normally remains vague and imprecise. . . . The cure interrelates these opposite poles, facilitating the transition from one to the other, and demonstrates, within a total experience, the coherence of the psychic universe, itself a projection of the social universe."[11] Possession, whether voluntary or involuntary, broaches the barrier between matter and essence; it attacks the capacity of knowledge to distinguish inner from outer, good from evil, even noumena from phenomena.

Immiscibles abut here in the possessed and destructured consciousness which reverses incarnation and parodies transcendence. Yet even at its most violent this negation indicates something not to be abandoned; even in ruins the subject is valuable; even then it becomes the evidence that value might be stipulated and chosen, that structure might assert itself over chaos. The desperate and equally violent forces of inquisition and exorcism make this clear: they follow possession into the body's space to contest and reclaim both the details and the unity of discourse; they repossess structure by opposing demonic randomness, whose signs are those of a busy but purposeless magpie, "horse-dung, needles, feathers, hair, balls of thread, bits of glass, an iron knife a span long, egg-shells, mussel shells, and the like." They offer instead the "formidable ceremony" of exorcism. And "there must always be witnesses."[12] The ceremony is as public and as reconstituting as marriage; for what is implied by possession, that denial of the subject's will to choose

10. René Girard, *Violence and the Sacred*, trans. Patrick Gregory (Baltimore, 1977), 317, 51.

11. Claude Lévi-Strauss, "The Sorcerer and His Magic," in his *Structural Anthropology*, trans. Claire Jakobson and Brooke Grundfest Schoepf (New York, 1967), 177.

12. H. C. Lea, *Materials Toward a History of Witchcraft*, ed. Arthur C. Howland (3 vols.; New York, 1957), III, 1047, 1066, 1064–65.

freely under law, is the entire space within the network of systematic differentiation, everything that man had achieved by the generative exclusion of the first ritual victim, by the "mechanism which, in a single decisive moment, curtails reciprocal violence and imposes structure on the community."[13] Possession is the force by which an excluded other furiously retrieves its mastery: it marks the return of an immense power which was turned out, wholly separated, in spite of itself, from the discourse that it originally governed.

It is useful to propose, then, that possession enables us to explore the function of signs (a much more fundamental question, but related to the structure of possession) in the broadest possible manner. To put it less abstractly, James's use of the theme of possession may allow us to infer his intentions in developing a new language for realism. For James, that is, possession served as a means of learning how to understand not only the surface but the history and structure of reality in an accurate mode. It demands the inquisition of its signs not as objects but as the evidence of an excluded ideality which aims to reclaim them. Possession was interesting and important to him because it stressed the doubleness of knowledge, and because it illuminated boundaries so clearly. Yvor Winters has spoken of the efforts of James and his characters "to understand ethical problems in a pure state, and to understand them absolutely, to examine the marginal, the semiobscure, the fine and definitive boundary of experience . . . the moral divorced from all problems of manners and of compulsion, as it appears in the case of Fleda Vetch."[14] Possession demands precisely this inquisitorial understanding of a region which is both frontier and barrier for the soul, and James saw the theme into the bargain as a struggle for power that enforced exactly appropriate demands on the literary sign, which, like all signs during an epoch of epistemic inflection, undergoes considerable transformation. It is as if signs themselves experience a similar struggle for possession: as if they focus a violent juxtaposition of conflicting references, a conflation in which

13. Girard, *Violence and the Sacred*, 317.
14. Yvor Winters, "Maule's Well, or Henry James and the Relation of Morals to Manners," in his *In Defense of Reason* (Denver, n.d.), 338.

opposite modes of reality are allowed to interpenetrate one another, the border separating related opposites becomes permeable, and reality thus to a certain extent not only appears but gradually becomes a different place.

Perhaps the theme of possession points to such a transformation of the sign, to a restructuration of meaning; perhaps possession, for James, is a way of representing the struggle of the sign to transform itself according to the new mode of signifying called realism, which also examined the limits of romantic mystification. Perhaps even it is not too much to suggest that possession is a trace of the signified; that it had come to stand for the romantic power of essences and ideation, repressed and lost thanks to the realist effort to overcome romantic figuration and its understanding. Here the force of romanticism—the engulfment of perceptions by feelings and attitudes, or perhaps a desire to escape quotidian life into a passionate difference—is faced by James's scheme for the text, which represents that power as a variety of appetites: the publishing scoundrel of *The Aspern Papers,* say, or the ghost that haunts an old house or portrait. It becomes, as it is demystified, a perilous motive for understanding and commitment; a haunted realm beyond the brute specifications of sense, which, if it is not faced with the fullest power of self-knowledge, becomes a demonic energy, the dark side of repressed spirit, a ghostly possession of the text.

So Jamesian possession may dramatize a realignment in the whole process of signification. It is axiomatic that in James (and the other realists) one finds traditional literary language, that formal and sedimented order, changing as the dimension of concept and belief undergoes its own important change. The balance of the sign shifts; and it is doubtless a measure of the anxiety and uncertainty associated with this profound change (which after all entailed the repudiation of an immense theological system) that the idea of possession should so aptly express the relationship. Nothing less than the phenomenal and noumenal orders oppose one another across the frontier that associates and distinguishes them within the tense system of each sign. The incursion of noumena into phenomena, the incarnation of spirit within flesh, the possession of one independent realm by another—with drastic and ramifying realignments of power implied—all these problems are drawn into the discovery of a new literary mode suited to a diminished influence of the signified's province, of spiritual or ideal allusion.

The work of the nineties, then, insofar as it is typified in *Poynton,* may be understood to develop the literary sign by exploring possession. Characters are immersed in an atmosphere of evil, which is generally the attempt of corrupting possessive powers to annex a method of knowledge. Whether or not this possession is explicitly demonic its structure is consistent. James nominated them the "hovering prowling blighted presences" in his Preface to "The Turn of the Screw"; in the Preface to *What Maisie Knew* his figure is the "infected air" in which Maisie "vibrates." In the Preface to *The Altar of the Dead* he speaks of "some imaged appeal of the lost Dead," a "hauntedness" that threatens "as incessantly as forked lightning may play unheeded about the blind"; in the Notes for *The Sense of the Past* of an "ancient brutality," a "liability" which seems "to hover and to menace."[15] Maisie, the Governess, May Bartram, Fleda: each of these haggard spirits is menaced by some possessive presence which seeks to overpower the possibility of free utterance that they represent.

Unhappily for them, the menaces of possession are made to seem irresistibly alluring. They consist, for example, of a dazzling collection or a beautiful museum shadowed by barren, powerful forces; a brilliant agglomeration of inherited things, a haunted lovely house or perfect friend whose value is qualified by some immovable obstacle to understanding. Possession is what Fleda first delightedly sees as "a future full of the things she particularly loved" (11), but this is a blandishment of choices always already made, signs whose meaning and arrangement are always already ordained by an older order. This is the full structure of James's "real": a desperate hazard of options working free of that allure of mystifying attitudes and texts: selection resisting possession. Is it an obsolete and romantic order of signs which inheres in the anthology of beauty at Poynton? and which returns, in Mrs. Gereth, to possess the space from which it has been excluded? Certainly one might propose such a reading

15. James, *The New York Edition,* XII, xx, XI, xiv, XVII, v, XXVI, 309, 311, 312.

of "The Turn of the Screw" or *The Sense of the Past,* or of *What Maisie Knew* or of *Poynton,* in all of which some possessive claim menaces an independent struggle freely to understand the fullest scope of reality and one's own claim on it.

The plot of *The Spoils of Poynton* is simple. Fleda Vetch, a young woman "whose only treasure was her subtle mind" (13), meets, during a weekend at the vulgar estate Waterbath, the widowed Mrs. Gereth, also a guest, with whom she shares a loathing of the varnish and cheap curios there assaulting their taste. Mrs. Gereth has collected the magnificent antiques assembled at her own estate, Poynton Park; but under the terms of her recently deceased husband's will both estate and collection pass to their son, Owen, a pleasant blockhead whose unfortunate liaison with Mona Brigstock, a daughter of Waterbath, eventually results in marriage. Mrs. Gereth, appalled by the danger that the spoils of Poynton might fall into these heavy hands, tries to arrange an attachment of Fleda and Owen, and this interesting possibility develops; but Fleda, though passionately in love with Owen and ravished by the spoils now in his possession (upon first seeing Poynton "her meagre past fell away from her like a garment of the wrong fashion" [11]—she is much like the Governess), insists that Mona should set him free before she herself will hear a promise from him.

Mona, however, like Mrs. Gereth, is an agent of possession rather than freedom. As Professor Banta says, "the cleverly stupid Mona with her monomaniacal will thwarts the fine and vulnerable intelligence of Fleda Vetch," and this is an example of "the possession by the self of what is not the self."[16] Mona insists, naturally, on a full inventory of the objects at Poynton simply because they are legally part of her prospects as the future Mrs. Gereth (she has no feeling for them per se), and she regards Owen, perhaps, as only another such object. In an evil hour she seduces the young man to reaffirm his engagement to her, marries him forthwith, and becomes proprietress of the spoils. These Mrs. Gereth, who is a kind of vampire herself, has first antagonistically carried away to the dower house set aside for her under the will, and then returned pre-

---

16. Banta, *Henry James and the Occult,* 85, 83.

maturely to let Owen understand her willingness to surrender them to such a doyenne as Fleda. Both Fleda and Mrs. Gereth end by being cast out rather than endowed. They lose their claim on the spoils, and Owen; upon arriving at Poynton to claim a parting gift from him—a Maltese cross, by all accounts the prize piece of the collection—Fleda finds that the entire estate has been destroyed by fire.

This leaves her, futureless as she is, the unwilling parasite of Mrs. Gereth, whose companion in nostalgia for the lost signs she has become. She is essentially placeless, like Maisie and the Governess among so many others; she is free of any complicity to set possession against the freedom to choose for oneself, but the price of this is alienation and subservience—at that, preferable to the implied corruption of possession. Most critics have understood Fleda's ethical struggle to be James's chief interest in the novel.[17] Certainly this question may be said to remain ambiguous and important, but it seems to me to stop short of representing James's text at its most complex or interesting. Clearly *The Spoils of Poynton* concerns itself with her problem of possession, as well as her difficulty of choice. The contested spoils preside over the text. They signify and determine not only the scope of Fleda's ethical responsibility but her desire to claim Owen freely—and Mona's to possess him herself; and Mrs. Gereth's interest in her son's dependence, which shadows Fleda's urgent commitment to the independent will. The spoils are the general signs onto which the novel's specific representations of erotic will and possession are displaced; they become the alibi of desire.

Possession of the spoils, and of the claimants who contend for them, therefore focuses the problem of meaning in the novel. Indeed they come to represent a radical alteration not only of mean-

17. See, for instance, James W. Gargano, "*The Spoils of Poynton:* Action and Responsibility," *Sewanee Review,* LXIX (1961), 650. *Cf.* Alan H. Roper, "The Moral and Metaphorical Meaning of *The Spoils of Poynton,*" *American Literature,* XXXII (1960), 182–96; Edmund L. Volpe, "The Spoils of Art," *Modern Language Notes,* LXXIV (1959), 323–43; and John C. Broderick, "Nature, Art, and Imagination in *The Spoils of Poynton,*" *Nineteenth-Century Fiction,* XII (1959), 295–312. The best general discussion of the aesthetics of this novel is Gary D. Trotter's "The Process of Selection in Henry James" (Ph.D. dissertation, State University of New York at Buffalo, 1979).

ing but of the evaluation and structure of meaning. Once, human will struggled to create them, these "great syllables of colour and form, the tongues of other countries and the hands of rare artists" (22). They resemble the debris of an original language. But even more they express Mrs. Gereth's "strange, almost maniacal disposition to thrust in everywhere the question of 'things,' to read all behavior in the light of some fancied relation to them" (24)—all behavior, not only the tasteful appreciation of cognoscenti but also the responses of any opposing will to her possession: her husband's testament, her son's erotic interests, Fleda's power of ethical discernment and choice. They are doubtless, each one, of a singular beauty and interest. Each piece carries a dim echo of its own history somewhere within it; Fleda "knew them by the personal name their distinctive sign or story had given them" (73). But neither history nor knowledge is really apparent, to us at least; it remains one of the novel's secrets. The beauty of their origin has given way to their recent history and even more to the problem of ownership or control. Mr. Gereth's will has managed, by putting Owen's ownership above his mother's, to grant his heir the bare possibility of freedom, an end to (maternal) possession. It gives him the option to begin again, since it poses a possible freedom from her mania to valorize and sustain the signs of a lost and obsolete order. This is not unlike the promise of Huck's freedom from Tom, or Isabel Archer's from Osmond, or, perhaps, Dreiser's freedom from the law of sentiment. It offers some faint hope of origination, an escape from the oedipal shadow—that replication of an old desire.

So a struggle for possession adds its energy to their original meaning and even to their beauty; "each history of each find, each circumstance of each capture" inheres in them as Mrs. Gereth and Fleda review the rooms at Poynton: "The shimmer of wrought substances spent itself in the brightness; the old golds and brasses, old ivories and bronzes, the fresh old tapestries and deep old damasks threw out a radiance in which the poor woman now saw in solution all her old loves and patiences, all her old tricks and triumphs" (58). They spend themselves, their exhaustion is both sexual and commercial, and in this instance it is Mrs. Gereth whose obsolete values and principle of order they function to display. These signs are not limited to their first historical significance, which was the representation of a spiritual or political value, or even to their second, which is that of the explosion of those values regathered at Poynton. They have become (this is repeatedly emphasized) the signs of Mrs. Gereth's assembly and possession, of another order of representation which salvages fragments in order to integrate a life. She preserves, by the force of her will, not a lost historical event or epoch but the priority of her own obstinate possession. The signs she gathers she revalues, puts back together under new auspices. Arbitrary, narcissistic, her obsession works to reassert authority. From the scene of history she turns to the scene of desire; the power of the will eludes her; it has opened a range of options to desire—it restores the freedom of signs (gestures and stirrings as well as beautiful objects) to express meaning outside the closed circle of her own referral; it threatens her possession of meaning—her occupation of the space of signs. She stands for the real spirit of old meanings, a single dictation of significance which displaces the vulgarity of choice, the freedom to choose, whether foolishly or well, for oneself.

Collected from all the partitioned empires of Europe, almost entirely invisible to us as images though relentlessly pressing upon the perceptions of the characters, what, more precisely, might these spoils mean? In their places they make "a steady shining light" (321). Selecting among them is a matter of "comparing incomparables" (57); for Mrs. Gereth, "There wasn't a thing in the house she didn't like best" (50). As she says to Owen, then to Fleda, "The best things here, as you know, are the things your father and I collected. . . . there are things in the house that we almost starved for! They were our religion, they were our life, they were *us*! And now they're only me—except that they're also *you*, thank God, a little, you dear. . . . they're like living things to me" (30–31). This is of course her melodrama, a frenzied offer to share the spoils in order to bring Fleda, and through her Owen, and then through him the spoils once again, back under her control. But even though they occasion such remarkable frenzy they remain vague to us. They are "the glow of a Venetian lamp . . . a small but splendid tapestry" (70), "the touch of an old velvet brocade, a wondrous texture," a "great Italian cabinet" (971), and the Maltese cross, a small but marvellous crucifix of ivory, a masterpiece of delicacy, of expression and of the great Spanish period, the existence and precarious accessibility of which she had heard of at Malta, years before, by an odd and romantic chance—a clue followed through mazes of secrecy till the treasure was at last unearthed. (73–74)

But this is not an objectification of value, and just barely recalls a historical time. James is scarcely precise even in the instance of this best single masterpiece, which for us is at most small and ivory. These objects, all of them, despite their incomparable aesthetic value, have lost their objectivity; they are always on the verge of becoming subjective. However James means, in his treatment of the spoils, to make these signs meaningful, he always ends by showing that a reader can evaluate them only as a question of the relationship between objective and subjective reality which he deliberately vexes here and elsewhere.

All along Fleda, on the other hand, has known the objects, and the people she meets as well, neither objectively nor as a connoisseur but "by direct inspiration." Her intelligence is anything but superficial; it is, like all inspiration, deep and disturbing. "To be clever meant to know the 'marks'" (138); that is, the author-ity, superficially inscribed but also concealed, which identifies an original value. But Fleda's cleverness is greater yet. She has always had "to look straight at realities and fill out blanks" (140). She can understand the spoils as intrinsically rather than referentially valuable, quite unrelated to any conceivable currency. For her, nothing need be possessed: her goal is self-possession, the self knowing its own essence. Upon first seeing Poynton she dissolves in tears, "the natural and usual sign of her submissiveness to perfect beauty" (21). It is like a conversion experience; she is not so unlike Mary Scudder. "To give it all up, to die to it—that thought ached in her breast" (23). In the event, she finds herself the only hope to keep the vision of Poynton intact. But that will mean the self's possession by another. To win Owen from Mona will win Poynton (and Owen) for Mrs. Gereth. It is as simple and as complicated as that. But Owen, being engaged to Mona, is not free to respond to any such opportunity, however delectable it might seem to him: and for Fleda to be satisfied, Mona must freely give him up so that he may freely choose his new option.

Meanwhile the primary task (Fleda's love remains secret for some time) is that of negotiating possession of the great collection for Mrs. Gereth—ostensibly, to keep it away from the philistine Brigstocks, "from whose composition the principle of taste had been extravagantly omitted. In the arrangement of their home some other principle, remarkably active, but uncanny and obscure, had operated instead" (6). Waterbath is "perversely full of souvenirs of places even more ugly than itself" (7). It reverses Poynton: it celebrates imitation where Poynton seeks to recuperate an original wholeness. It is "an aesthetic misery" (9); it is "the presence of the dreadful"—not taste but "a universal futility" governs its assembly. It is "an ugliness fundamental and systematic" (6): "There were advantages enough," James points out, which "it clearly didn't possess" (3), and it too means to seize them, this uncanny and obscure principle (as keen an appetite as Mrs. Gereth's), in Poynton.

In such grossly empirical custody Poynton must fail of its design, and this specter sometimes makes Fleda think, of Mrs. Gereth's intense determination, that "it was not the crude love of possession; it was the need to be faithful to a trust and loyal to an idea" (46). But her problem is much more complex than this. Fleda finds herself the mediator of a struggle for possession that functions on several levels, each to some extent corrupt, and all working against her own determination to find relationships that are not possessive at all. Thus her own acceptance of Poynton's values, which has always been contingent, soon becomes overdetermined.[18] No simple exchange is possible when the status of signs is so vexed, because no exchange is free from the problem of despoilment. This disorder in the system of exchange is exemplified by the difficulties of erotic relationship in the novel, which are invariably possessive struggles in one way or another.

Though fascinated by the spoils to be sure, and Owen is doubtless one of them, Fleda wishes to possess nothing. But she is an insufficient agent of reciprocal freedom; her dilemma arises in her squalid dependence, a poverty so helpless that it makes her espe-

18. See Philip L. Greene, "Point of View in *The Spoils of Poynton,*" *Nineteenth-Century Fiction,* XXI (1967), 361.

cially vulnerable to possession. She is "a young lady without fortune and without talent" (148); she "had neither a home nor an
outlook—nothing in all the wide world but a feeling of suspense"
(145). Fleda, "with her mother dead, hadn't so much as a home"
(14). She is the perfect emblem (like so many of James's young
women) of a zero degree of meaning—inheriting nothing, owing
nothing. Her poverty makes her brilliantly free to choose without
considering old allegiances.[19] In this she is like many of the heroes
of our classic literature. The condition is ontological; it defines a
subjectivity which owes nothing (or as little as possible) to the romantic paradigm, that promise of emotional and spiritual riches, a
wealth, a superfluity and finally an imposition of meaning. In her
own way she struggles as ardently as Phoebe Pyncheon to be free.
Fleda attempts to hold open the possibility that signs, and the
whole structure of Culture, might be freshly chosen as well as fully
systematic. She wishes to preserve the freedom and order which the
spoils represent; she would enable, if she could, the ideal point of
orientation—the "perfect beauty," the "secret rapture" (260)—to
find its custody in perception and in flesh. Hers is the energy, the
arch of metaphor. But Fleda is a metaphor that fails.

Of course she fails. How could she succeed? The obverse of her
freedom from legacy is her susceptibility to donation. Fleda is
easily annexed, because she has nothing with which to reciprocate.
Mrs. Gereth "had made a desert round her, possessing and absorb-
ing her so utterly that other partakers had fallen away" (144)—virtually as if she were the substance of a private communion. For
others—"her kind little circle at large, who didn't now at all matter"—Fleda's "tendency had begun to define itself as parasitical"
(41): "people *were* saying that she fastened like a leech on other
people" (60). It must seem like that. But Fleda herself wonders,
when Mrs. Gereth requests her company on a long trip abroad, "if
this were not practically a demand for penal submission—for a
surrender that, in its complete humility, would be a long expia-
tion" (233). Their relationship tells us what has become of signs.
The two of them can manage only by admitting the hiatus in their

19. See Isle, *Experiments in Form*, 89.

life. Their companionship had "begun to shape itself almost wholly on breaches and omissions" (253); they exist under "the protection of suspended allusions" (257). They will live, one should imagine, a life barren of metaphor, there being no question of a perfect form or reciprocity to which their conversation might refer. Their art will be all evasion. Even the representation of the spoils is lost to them now. In dismissing the spoils the novel has also dismissed, as some texts do, "the possibility of restoring or re-constituting, beneath the metaphor which at once conceals and is concealed, what was 'originally represented.'"[20] And that original representation is, Mrs. Gereth says to Fleda, "what we don't, you know, by your wish, ever talk about" (256).

One chance does however remain that Fleda's life might be enriched by a sign. Some time after Owen's marriage she receives a letter which seems to her beyond interpretation—"it had mysteries for her that she couldn't meet. What did it mean, what did it represent, to what did it correspond in his imagination or his soul? What was behind it, what was before it, what was, in the deepest depth, within it?" (259). Such are the problems of understanding in her condition. But his motive does not seem so obscure. "I want you inexpressibly," he says, "to have as a remembrance something of mine—something of real value. Something from Poynton is what I mean. . . . I want you to take from me, and to choose for yourself . . . the thing in the whole house that's most beautiful and precious. I mean the 'gem of the collection,' don't you know? If it happens to be of such a sort that you can take immediate possession of it—carry it right away with you—so much the better" (258).

Poor gift, poor freedom now to choose! It is a sign of their loss of one another that he wishes her to select, though she cannot see that. After her loss Fleda's "obliterated passion" and the spoils are somehow given "to memory and to love" and she comes to believe that they were "nobody's at all—too proud, unlike base animals and humans, to be reducible by anything so narrow" as the idea of possession (235). But at last, after a long month—it is close to

20. Jacques Derrida, "White Mythology," trans. F. C. T. Moore, *New Literary History*, VI (1974), 8.

Christmas, that season of the narrative of Bly—she agrees with her-self to "go down to Poynton as a pilgrim might go to a shrine" (259). She will "act upon his offer" so as to "have as her own some-thing splendid that he had given her, of which the gift had been his signed desire." In this instance of visiting Poynton, she believes, "she should be able to say to herself that . . . her possession was as complete as that of either of the others whom it had filled only with bitterness" (260).

But as she leaves "it was spoiling for a storm" (261). The "dawn was dolorous," "the green fields were black, the sky was all alive with the wind," and something "had begun to press on her heart" (262). When she arrives, Poynton is in flames. Everywhere her vi-sion is obscure as smoke. In the swimming air she sees "something like the disc of a clock." History—the history once so lucidly as-sembled by the spoils—is reduced to this vague flat and circular image. Fleda covers her face with her hands; she "felt herself give everything up." Her options close; her life narrows to the one bitter choice—but it means, no doubt, that she will be possessed herself from now on: "I'll go back," she weakly says (266).

To Mrs. Gereth. And this returns Fleda to the will that first as-sembled the spoils. They are not merely acquired; they *are* pos-sessed, finally but not only by Owen's mother. They have been ap-propriated and reappropriated and bartered and so on until, like the Malta whose cross epitomizes them, they become the ground not of any inherent meaning of their own but the place of that fun-damental question of invasion and possession. To possess these signs, and Mona realizes this, is to achieve the custody of power, to realign desire and meaning. For Mona, possession of the spoils turns meaning from one mode to another. It reduces art, history, meaning, whatever the spoils have signified, to a question of per-sonality, a triumph of malice over system. But in this she only sec-onds Mrs. Gereth.

Or perhaps they first came into Mrs. Gereth's possession through her attempt to recuperate not only beauty but the order of Cul-ture—let us give the benefit of the doubt. Poynton is "all France and Italy with their ages composed to rest," and "England . . . was the wide embrace" (22). But this also makes Poynton the sar-

cophagus of desire, does it not? The sentence describing the day of
the fire is paradoxical in just this way. "The green fields were black,
the sky was all alive with the wind"—this language is literal and
figurative at the same time without privileging either aspect beyond
question; it suggests death, it suggests life; both are present at
once; to express a universe through such signs is to be poised, waiting for one or the other to determine not what was but what is real.
Fleda feels all this in losing Owen. Mrs. Gereth must feel something very similar in losing the spoils. They threaten, in passing
away from her as they do—into the possession of a rival, a barbar-
ian, a daughter-in-law—the absolute loss of her meaning: "In the
event of a surrender the poor woman would never again be able to
begin to collect: she was now too old and too moneyless, and times
were altered" (47). Not only the age of creation but that of con-
gregation has passed away.

So the collection is, or was, a dimension of power, an embrace
and a crypt signifying the imperial authority that Mrs. Gereth
chooses to replicate through her possession of its elegant detritus.
In a way her possession does preserve the sense of the past. The
fragments are the remnants of the obsolete empire which she has
claimed as her own: she becomes the monarch of the imperial
imagination she has appropriated. Mrs. Gereth is like the narcissistic prince of the "ostentatious Baroque tradition" whose pal-
aces have been described by Jean Starobinski. For such princes,
"the outward show, at least in its older form, was more than mere
show: it was a spectacle whose spectators were not to remain distant and objective; their freedom was lost in the captivating magic
of the scene; they were systematically bewitched into participa-
tion, into a ritual submission, in a magnificent demonstration of
the monarch's irresistible will. The ostentation was not simply the
sign of sovereignty: it was the expression of power externalized,
made perceptible to the senses, able to renew its outward manifestations indefinitely."[21] Poynton is, for Mrs. Gereth—and for

21. Jean Starobinski, *The Invention of Liberty*, trans. Bernard C. Swift (Geneva,
1964), 14.

Mona too—what Mark Girouard calls a "power house."[22] Such houses as these were signs of control: displays by those whose possession of political and ideological power followed a clear pattern from medieval times into the nineteenth century. The great house was "an image-maker, which projected an aura of glamour, mystery or success around its owner. It was visible evidence of his wealth. It showed his credentials" (3).

The possession of such a house by the Gereths—or, say, the difficulty which it represents as soon as it becomes a legacy—already reveals "a change in the power structure" (9), and a deep shift in the order of Culture. Waterbath puts that change in italics. These houses show that some "economic balance [had begun] to change" (2), to be sure, but the context of the change is complex, and the transformation is broadly ontological as well as social or economic; and clearly the great house is the house of fiction too. All of these signs exactly figure, as they change, a question of power—the power within the sign. "The personal relationship between the monarch and his domains," Starobinski observes, "was visible to the whole world: according to the myth of absolute power, the perception of this expansive glory should immediately transform the observer into a grateful subject, making him an integral element in the circle of royal possession" (14). In the case of a private patron, the owner "may himself determine what function the work shall have" (13); at least, she may struggle toward that end. In the case of Mrs. Gereth, the function is in fact more political than private; it is "the visible demonstration of sovereignty" (14) which represents absolute power. To be sure Poynton is a park, the sort of place in which the wealthy patron "wanted trees and greenery and a garden in which he could relax and muse freely, away from the petty obligations of official or social functions," but such patrons also needed "elegance, harmony, and a sense of imposing majesty" (49), for their own power was a representation too, a metaphor of princely authority: "The relationship between prince and court was as be-

22. Mark Girouard, *Life in the English Country House: A Social and Architectural History* (New Haven, 1978), 10. Subsequent references will be given parenthetically in the text.

tween possessor and possessed; and this constituted the analogical image of the relationship the prince desired between himself and the entire world" (14).

The perceived beauty of these objects is wholly subordinated, then, by the idea of political power (which is threatened in turn by Owen's marriage to an outsider). Were they ever merely the signs of his mother's nostalgic genius for assembling fragments? Or did they arrange the scattered aspects of a lost reality in the textual place of Poynton, which she has determined will shut out all possession and all desire but her own? In either case, in that space which is at once so coherent and so divided from any original or even represented meaning—that is, the space of Poynton Park, which is never more than the space of possession for us—a new structure is constituted, and an old one destroyed. Poynton Park, though we see it only inferentially, through the struggle that transmogrifies objective representation into subjective expression, is the irradiating place of the sign's fission. Here the sign redefines itself; here possession—ideological, erotic, demonic, possession as enforcement, as a question of law, politics, desire, theology—here all these senses of possession convene on Poynton, and in the texts of the nineties, to provide for an exploration of the process by which reality is signified.

All James's tales of possession and haunting, including *The Spoils of Poynton,* are like the séance in "Maud-Evelyn," which depends on "the aid not only of the few small, cherished relics, but that of the fondest figments and fictions, ingenious imaginary mementoes and tokens, the unexposed make-believe of the sorrow that broods and the passion that clings."[23] This is the scene of possession, both spiritual and erotic; these are the memorials of desire, the values transcending interrogation or analysis—a realm beyond merely pragmatic texts. They reveal a characteristic Jamesian tint, the need and longing for an order outside empirical experience. The power of romanticism had sought to privilege that lost dimension, which realism repudiated. What James sought to express was the value

23. Leon Edel (ed.), *The Complete Tales of Henry James* (12 vols.; London, 1964), XI, 59.

not of romantic art but of the signified, a dimension in which meaning might recognize the priority of essence as well as object, and which had been diminished by the rejection of the romantic code. His fiction follows the lost order of the signified as it struggles to find its way back into meaning through tokens and fragments, seeking to possess the scene from which it had been cast out.

James's interest in this problem leads to the advance in realist aesthetics which he developed as no one else did. It is a revision of things he accomplishes, and he works against a trend. His friend Howells, by any account one of the chief arbiters of the realist movement, praised Hamlin Garland for his "fine courage to leave a fact with the reader, ungarnished and unvarnished." Garland expressed his irritation at "the aloofness of fiction and poetry from the realities of common life and speech," *common* being a sort of catchword which indicated a factual reality that remained free of the glaze of imperative attitudes. Harold Frederic advised Gertrude Atherton to "listen with a more solicitous, reflective ear—and get the trick of drawing *sound* out of the ink-bottle!" Clemens wrote of *Joan of Arc* that it satisfied by being "mere history—history pure and simple—history stripped naked of flowers, embroideries, colorings, exaggerations, inventions." James himself, early on, complained that though Hawthorne "had a high sense of reality . . . he never attempted to render exactly or closely the actual facts of the society that surrounded him." And Dreiser, though he saw vague "forces" abstractly at work in the universe, concluded "I take no meaning from life other than the picture it presents to the eye—the pleasure and pain it gives to the body."[24]

But James expresses his aesthetic more generously, perhaps, when, five years later, in "The Art of Fiction," he speaks of the way

24. Howells quoted in Harrison T. Messerole *et al.* (eds.), in *American Literature: Tradition and Innovation* (2 vols.; Lexington, Mass., 1969), IV, 2082; Hamlin Garland, *Roadside Meetings* (New York, 1930), 90. From a letter in my possession: Harold Frederic to Gertrude Atherton, July 10, 1898. Atherton preserved the letter in her copy of Frederic's *Illumination* (the British title of *The Damnation of Theron Ware*). Lewis Leary (ed.), *Mark Twain's Correspondence with Henry Huttleston Rogers, 1893–1909* (Berkeley, 1969), 124; Henry James, *Hawthorne* (Ithaca, 1956), 98; Theodore Dreiser, *Dawn* (New York, 1931), 588.

a contemporary writer "converted . . . ideas into a concrete image and produced a reality": "The power to guess the unseen from the seen, to trace the implication of things, to judge the whole piece by the pattern, the condition of feeling life in general so completely that you are well on your way in knowing any particular corner of it—this cluster of gifts may almost be said to constitute experience." Howells too commented at greater length in *Criticism and Fiction,* where he predicted that "when realism becomes false to itself, when it heaps up facts merely, and maps life instead of picturing it, realism will perish."[25]

The goal realism sought was that of restoring to literature what James called (in "The Art of Fiction") "solidity of specification," what Howells (in *Criticism and Fiction*) meant to demand when he said "let fiction cease to lie about life; let it portray men and women as they are, actuated by the motives and passions in the measure we all know" (104). But realism had had to begin by expelling an obsolete tradition of the signified from literary language. It had had to learn how to privilege the brute details that Crane (in "The Open Boat") called "the furniture of the world."[26] Once that lesson was learned, it became necessary to rediscover an authentic access to the power of the signified, however, because no language, literary or otherwise, can conceivably function without a coherent noumenal power.

James's use of his ghostly themes, especially the theme of possession, addresses exactly this problem. Possession represents the ghost, as it were, of romanticism, which the realist impulse had excluded from the text and which, as an incoherent order of the signified, is hauntingly searching for readmission to discourse. Possession is the voice of metaphysics exorcised by a logic which chooses to emphasize the unvarnished fact as the basis of a literary movement. But the theme of possession has an ontological as well as a historical status; it serves the larger question of the structure of the

25. Henry James, "The Art of Fiction," in his *Partial Portraits* (New York, 1968), 389, 390; William Dean Howells, *Criticism and Fiction* (New York, 1892), 15–16. Subsequent references will be given parenthetically in the text.

26. James, "The Art of Fiction"; Stephen Crane, *The Open Boat,* in Robert Wooster Stallman (ed.), *Stephen Crane: Stories and Tales* (New York, 1955), 230.

reality which it represents; and from this perspective the motif of possession poses an ominous threat—that noumena might regain the power which had delivered reality into the custody of metaphysical illusion. How to find a legitimate basis for the possessive impulse—how to find an accurate metaphor which would express the need for the signified (and its legitimate claims) while neutralizing its theological reference: this was James's dilemma. Without a solution, it is possible to argue, no literary mode can complete itself.

Roland Barthes, speaking of Jules Michelet's *La sorcière,* notes Michelet's definition of the possessed personality as one which is "excluded from the world and necessary to the world," one who is seeking a "correction of reality."[27] Jamesian possession might well be put in these terms. It clarifies an obscure language, one haunted by a force which, though it has lost its mastery, nonetheless means to insist on an irreducible unity of form and meaning—the structure of the sign. That structure has been jeopardized by a romantic crisis of signification and is here inscribing the limit of the realist effort to demystify. This crisis certainly suggests "an anxiety of language," in a phrase of Derrida's, which occurs at the point where "the simple significative nature of language appears rather uncertain, partial, or inessential," so that the form of fiction (say) is like "a city no longer inhabited, not simply left behind, but haunted by meaning and culture."[28]

If one prefers historical rather than theoretical argument there is Peter Brooks's fine essay, which develops the idea of a "moral occult"—that "domain of operative spiritual values which is both indicated within and masked by the surface of reality . . . not a metaphysical system [but] a realm which in quotidian existence may appear closed off from us, but which we . . . must get in touch with since it is the realm of meaning and value." James and Balzac (with whom Brooks links James) reject, on the one hand—so Brooks argues—"any metaphysical reduction of real life, and refuse to re-

27. Roland Barthes, *"La sorcière,"* in his *Critical Essays,* trans. Richard Howard (Evanston, 1972), 114.
28. Jacques Derrida, "Force and Significance," in his *Writing and Difference,* trans. Alan Bass (Chicago, 1978), 3, 4, 5.

duce their metaphysical enterprise to the cold symbolism of allegory." What had James said?—"Hawthorne, in his metaphysical moods, is nothing if not allegorical, and allegory, to my sense, is quite one of the lighter exercises of the imagination." On the other hand, Brooks goes on, James and Balzac "refuse to allow that the world has been drained of transcendence; and they locate that transcendence in the struggle of the children of light with the children of darkness, in the play of ethical mind."[29] This is a struggle taking place within language—the dramatic struggle of meaning with form: of signified and signifier, spirit and matter. Language cannot exclude it; language is always haunted, always possessed. Nowhere in literary realism is this struggle of language so fully or so usefully made a problem of meaning as in James's narratives of possession.

29. Peter Brooks, "The Melodramatic Imagination: The Example of Balzac and James," in David Thorburn and Geoffrey Hartman (eds.), *Romanticism: Vistas, Instances, Continuities* (Ithaca, 1973), 203, 210; James, *Hawthorne*, 49.

Touring the Ruins

I looked at her then to see if I could discern traces of what I had seen in the beginning. There were traces but only traces. Vestiges. Hints of a formerly intact mystery never to be returned to its original wholeness. "I know what you're doing," she said, "you are touring the ruins."

—Donald Barthelme,
"Critique de la Vie Quotidienne"

American fiction develops toward the isolation and suppression of erotic desire—toward Fleda Vetch, who loses the beloved's magic to transform. Carrie at least has her illusions, but Fleda is left with no metaphors, not even the ambiguous association of language and morality by which Ben Halleck sustains the crisis of his desire for Marcia Hubbard. Fleda is less even than her father. Mr. Vetch, alone in his rooms, has (if nothing else) "the objects he was fond of saying he had collected—objects, shabby and battered, of a sort that appealed little to his daughter: old brandy-flasks and match-boxes, old calendars and hand-books, intermixed with an assortment of penwipers and ash-trays, a harvest gathered from the penny bazaars."[1] But these are of a kind with Carrie's images of transit—the detritus of consumption: drink, tobacco, time that has passed, lights gone out, obsolete guides and directions, the remains not of texts but of blotted pens. From Poynton to the dower house at Ricks to her father's flat in West Kensington, in the descent that precedes the loss once and for

1. Henry James, *The Spoils of Poynton* (New York, 1909), 145, Vol. X of *The New York Edition of Henry James,* 26 vols. Subsequent references will be given parenthetically in the text.

all of a future in desire, Fleda tours the ruins of a world signified at every stage by the structure of possession—by the metaphor which, in her fine commitment to a free choice for the future, she can only wish to escape. "It didn't matter what she collected," her father assures her; "she would find it gave an interest to life" (145); but Fleda's tragedy is that she must look to the capital of life, not to any such interest, not to the economy which saves and hoards and banks. She already knows, in her "short wild gusts of despair" (146), what Strether learns at long last: life cannot be invested; it must be lived (Strether says to the fullest) through oneself, spent not in a glance to the past but in those moments of commitment and choice which Isabel Archer and Maggie Verver learn to privilege, and which John Marcher defers and denies.

It is transformation, the opposite of possession, that Fleda struggles and fails to achieve; and in her failure she marks, once and for all and as some other late nineteenth-century characters do, the end of desire as a means of grace. Owen is too thick, she is too vulnerable; the ancient metaphors of possession, legal or romantic, are too strong for her. Breaking free of the clutter and force of the old meanings, making reality new, is not so easy. The medium of language itself was possessed; so was the space of the sign; and if the universe of possession had no future, if "times were altered and good things impossibly dear" (147), possession had nonetheless become all the more furious and determined; and the house of fiction, though lost to one vision, had not quite (for James, at any rate) been realized by a new one: "Poynton's *gone?*" Fleda asks the stationmaster, and he falters, then replies: "What can you call it, Miss, if it ain't really saved?" (266).

So Fleda's fullest goal, the house as an unencumbered legacy of choices, resembles Carrie's appetite for things, and Marcia's devouring piety, in becoming an ironic negation of desire. Her fine will yields to the obstinate resistance of her demons. The freedom of erotic choice she seeks and offers is canceled by the problem of an absolute ownership—by Mrs. Gereth and by Mona Brigstock, who stand for the possession of signs by the will to stipulate, rather than set free. Fleda is one who initiates the motif spelled out by Bernard Malamud fifty years later, in another story about desire and an obstinate difference: "The language of the heart either is a dead language or else nobody understands it the way you speak it."[2] And Donald Barthelme takes as a major theme this disintegration both of the idea and the image of transforming desire: "As a flower moves toward the florist," he writes, "women turn toward men who are not good for them. Self-actualization is not to be achieved in terms of another person, but you don't know that, when you begin."[3]

These sentiments also express two of the greatest fictional bodies of work in twentieth-century America, Faulkner's and Updike's. Drusilla Sartoris and young Bayard, Joe Christmas and Joanna Burden, Jason and Quentin, Benjy, Ike McCaslin; and Rabbit Angstrom; these are characters who suffer and express desire in the root meaning of the word, the meaning of what is absent or lost. They represent a vision which "teaches us to look at the world no longer with the eyes of a confessor, a physician, or of God . . . but with the eyes of a man walking in his city with no other horizon but the spectacle before him, no other power than that of his own eyes."[4]

Updike's novel *The Witches of Eastwick,* for instance, shows us the horizon of New England, and the spectacle of our own recent history, as a scene of fashions, ephemeral signs, desires as transitory as fashions, desires which are dreams and rumors and whose claim on reality or intention is tenebrous, obscure, as fragile as memory. Indeed nothing but memories of the spectacle remain to constitute a reality beyond the vision of a moment. "What is of interest," Updike says, "is what our minds retain, what our lives have given to the air." What we have seen is what we get. The three witches whose fears and powers express the anxiety of the American 1960s "are gone, vanished; we were just an interval in their lives, and they in ours." The facts which might clarify the meaning of their restless desire are as lost as the texts in Hawthorne's Manse, "buried in vaults and drawers of old paperwork, silted over." Nothing arches

2. Bernard Malamud, "Black Is My Favorite Color," in his *Idiots First* (New York, 1966), 19.

3. Donald Barthelme, "The Rise of Capitalism," in his *Sixty Stories* (New York, 1981), 208.

4. Roland Barthes, "Objective Literature," in his *Critical Essays,* trans. Richard Howard (Evanston, 1972), 24.

beyond, nothing transforms: the meaning of a desire only gives way to new longings. Yet something lingers to haunt our vision with a possible meaning, "something oblong and invisible and exciting we do not understand." This meaning dissipates; it cannot be verified; like a spell, it seeks a power beyond the horizon, like a blur beyond the image in a mirror. Is our desire a metaphor of something more, after all? For Updike it is always there, this need to confront desire with its own hidden meaning, the possible shadow which is what we really sense as lost or missing—that history is more than the sum of our urges, that desire is a sign of something beyond itself; something: "It is there when we walk the beach in off-season" (like Hawthorne along the margin), "and the Atlantic in its blackness mirrors"—as for Mary Scudder, or for Carrie?—"the dense packed gray of the clouds: a scandal, life like smoke rising twisted into legend."[5]

Nevertheless Updike knows too that the urge toward metaphor, the coupling instinct, develops in our fiction toward a submission to spectacle; it mirrors a horizon of objects which it does not quite master or transcend. Rabbit Angstrom is the perfect instance of this tendency away from transforming desire. Rabbit is locked into the horizon of spectacle, the town of Mt. Judge, a world he can move in but never escape. Trying one night to leave his wife, looking for elsewhere—his goal is "the huge white sun of the South," "orange groves and smoking rivers and barefoot women," where he can "wake up with the stars above perfectly spaced in perfect health"—Rabbit finds that his road "narrows not so much by plan as naturally, the edges crumbling in." Rabbit is trapped by the field of his movement, which is always along one plane. Neither map nor territory will yield to his search for a different kind of place. "The land refuses to change. The more he drives the more the region resembles the country around Mt. Judge." Whether in flight from desire or toward it, and he is always in one or the other, "the further he drives the more he feels some great confused system . . . reaching for him."[6]

Entrapment: no way out of this intransigent form; no arc for his

5. John Updike, *The Witches of Eastwick* (New York, 1984), 343.
6. John Updike, *Rabbit, Run* (New York, 1960), 29, 25, 34, 31.

energy. Named for an imperceptible unit of measurement—one ten-millionth of a millimeter—Rabbit Angstrom records the cadence of reality broken down to the barest theoretical fragment, reassembling over and over into the same image (and always about to break down again) of repeated longing to escape the horizon. In Rabbit we are just this side of zero. What we see in him, in the Angstrom unit as in Fleda or Carrie or Marcia, is the misery of desire at odds with the arc toward meaning. For Rabbit the place of desire is "a whole world half-seen in the corner of his eye snuffed out."[7] In his first novel, in his first flight, enchanted by the idea of escape into difference, carried by Route 100 toward Delaware, Rabbit "wonders what it's like to make it to a Du Pont," or more exactly (his erotic imagination provides a context) "A barefoot Du Pont. Brown legs probably, bitty birdy breasts. Beside a swimming pool in France. Something like money in a naked woman, deep, millions." But already this road "begins to feel like part of the same trap"—the tracery of local highways drawing him into "a smothering hole where you can't move without killing somebody." The names on his road map become a limit rather than a promise when he "sees the map whole, a net, all those red lines and blue lines and stars, a net he is somewhere caught in."[8] By the end of his trilogy, on his way home from a broken vacation, "descending over Maryland and Delaware"—coming back from the south he once sought as an escape—Rabbit thinks again, more than twenty years later, of "rich women with little birdy breasts," but now the context is closed to desire, and even to pleasure. Now its metaphor is aggression or condescension carried to its furthest extreme, the objectification of the other. The scene is a spectacle: the women are "wearing tall black boots"; they are "in from the hunt. Walking past the butler into long halls past marble tables they flick with their whips." Now they are "women he will never fuck. He has risen as high as he can, the possibility of such women is falling from him, falling with so many other possibilities as he descends." His desire is always either a memory or a violation, or, with one lover (may be his last), "a void, a pure black box, a casket of perfect nothingness," a "noth-

7. John Updike, *Rabbit Is Rich* (New York, 1981), 462.
8. Updike, *Rabbit, Run,* 25, 36.

ingness seen by his single eye"; and he feels, finally, that "we are each of us filled with a perfect blackness."[9]

Gradually all our fiction develops toward this limit of desire, which is also the limit of the sign, or of meaning: the energy of desire and the identity of the sign, whether these are the threshold of essences or the agitated fractions of an intractable scene, follow the same route, turn together toward the spectacle of meaning, toward what the fleshly eye can see. At the center of the development is a powerful figure, certainly the most powerful developed by the novel: the erotic constellation, an arrangement of the signs of desire, within which satisfaction, shaping to one pattern or another of law, gradually and inexorably comes to judge or question its own value. This desire follows a pattern: it becomes a matter of alienation rather than transcendence, and this refers us to the whole text of meaning; the movement of desire expresses a revolution of signs, which is to say a shift at the heart and throughout the whole body of discourse, a tendency toward self-reference and self-interrogation.

But if something—transcendence—is lost, not all need be loss. The ruin of signs continues to offer a question; that is inherent in their structure; so they are the occasion of a new beginning too. The sign comes not to an emptiness but to a liquidation with which to oppose the iconography of form; to an admission of possibilities—a new basis for meaning which has learned, in the century between Hawthorne's Kenyon and Updike's Rabbit Angstrom, to give up the bare alternatives of euphoria and suffering, and to find other scenes of meaning for the desiring self. And this returns us to a beginning, to Barthes' "Where to Begin?": as he says, "The movement of analysis, in its endless process, is precisely to explode the text, the first cloud of meanings, the first image of content . . . not the text's truth but its *plural*": that is what the movement of analysis, of desire and of signs, has grown to face and to express: plurality, other modes of desire, inside the margins of the same word or name: open to choice.[10]

At the end of his story, for example, Rabbit's own longing seems

9. Updike, *Rabbit Is Rich*, 427–28, 417, 419, 425.
10. Roland Barthes, "Where to Begin?" in his *New Critical Essays,* trans. Richard Howard (New York, 1980), 89.

put to rest with the icons of desire. His life, the development of our fiction, the history of the sign all seem to have exhausted their part in the dismantling of this iconography. His world appears to be terminal. His vision is darkened by the growing sense of blackness and void toward which his desire has carried him. If there is a future or the promise of cadence in the various games that express Rabbit's *jouissance* it lies with his son's daughter; that is, in the sign of some other's desire. His son is "a hopeless loser" who has fled the "panic" of wife and child with his lover in search of elsewhere (like father like son), but a version of the old domestic scene opens to a new future which, if not exactly Rabbit's, seems about to take shape on the horizon of some other eyes. The infant, "oblong cocooned," without language but not without meaning, is put into Rabbit's arms as he watches the Super Bowl. She does not strain, like Bellini's infant, and he does not seize her—he is her body, and she is his. She too is a sign, "what he has been waiting for," what he can love without desiring: life to replace loss, light beyond perfect blackness, an original wholeness seen both as a trace and a beginning. She is a sign of herself but of his self too, of his senescence but of her promise. This is something beyond if not more than Barthelme's ruins, perhaps the beginning of a new cycle of desire. While Rabbit looks on, the nameless child "shows her profile blindly in the shuddering flashes of color jerking from the Sony." History is projected as the spectacle of the last game, every season's termination every season, shuddering, jerking—Rabbit's name has been his life, a stream of angst, but now the spectacle he sees is new, a sign in angstrom units. Watching the game as it assembles from these fragments of energy Rabbit Angstrom faces himself, at the end of a season but under the only conditions that allow another to begin: ruin; victory. Faces himself: she too is history in the Angstrom unit: "A real presence hardly weighing anything but alive. Fortune's hostage, heart's desire, a granddaughter. His. Another nail in his coffin. His."[11]

11. Updike, *Rabbit Is Rich*, 456, 459, 467. My colleague Stefan Fleischer has suggested the notion that Rabbit's name translates literally to "stream of angst."